Get Tough or Die

Get Tough or Die

Why I Forgave My Parents
for My Abusive Childhood

BARBARA L. SELLERS

Internet addresses given in this book were accurate at the time it went to press.

For reprint permission requests and special rate quantity sales, contact the publisher at: JenniferReich@MomosaPublishing.com or 610-216-0913.

Author's note: All of the stories in this book are true. Most of them are based on my own firsthand experiences, what I saw with my own eyes, notes I kept in a file for fifty years, and what I heard from family members and relatives. Some of my stories are told through the personal accounts of my brothers and sisters who were there and granted permission for me to quote them.

If I had questions about what happened, I contacted my siblings by phone and email to verify and confirm facts and details about what actually took place.

Not all twelve of us surviving children agree with every story or detail in my book, because every victim of child abuse sees things through a different set of eyes and handles their experiences in their own way.

To honor my siblings' right to privacy, I have changed their first names, except for those who are deceased or gave me permission to use their real first name, and no last names are used. I only hope all of my siblings, in turn, can respect my right to tell my story to honor our two sisters who died too young, and to help inspire others to stop spouse and child abuse.

Printed in the United States of America
Cover design by Christina Gaugler

Photo credits:
Page 21: Ma at age two: photographer unknown
Page 38: Ma and Pa's wedding photo: photographer unknown
Page 54: Family photo by Carson Photo Studio; bicycle photo by Gloria Morton
Page 76: Photo of two girls taken by Pa
Page 84: Aerial photo of the farm taken by the Pope County Tribune; photo of kids sitting in the corn and grain elevator taken by Kay Wells
Page 104: Both photos of matches and a threshing machine by Barbara L. Sellers
Page 122: Photo of the three children taken by Ethel Skoog
Page 134: Photos of Dr. Gordon Lee and Robert Letson, M.D. printed with permission from the Pope County Historical Society
Page 150: Photo of Martha taken by Barbara L. Sellers
Page 166: Photos taken by Vernon Photography Studio
Page 178: Photo of Joey and Missy by a shrine taken by Barbara L. Sellers
Page 194: Photos of awards all taken by Barbara L. Sellers; photo of Pat taken by Matil Rotter.

Library of Congress information available upon request.
ISBN 978-0-9844804-1-8

2 4 6 8 10 9 7 5 3 1 paperback

DEDICATION

I AM DEDICATING THIS BOOK to my sisters Katherine Lorraine and Martha Marie, who passed away at home without seeing a doctor. I believe they both might still be alive today if they had received the professional medical care they so richly deserved and needed. Unfortunately, they never had the chance to grow up, leave their abusive childhood environment, and live full and happy lives.

Katherine, I never met you because you passed away as a three-month-old infant about a year before I was born, but I saw photographs of you lying in your coffin in the living room of our farmhouse. You looked like a beautiful baby with dark, naturally curly hair, and I know you must now be one of the prettiest baby angels in Heaven.

Martha, when you suddenly passed away at nineteen, something died in me that day, too. I felt so drenched in grief that I became angry with God. It made no sense to me that you lived just long enough to suffer and die before you had a chance to know a better and happier life. At the time of your death, I wrote a poem called "The Wake." The last line read: *The purpose of your life I seek, but cannot find.* I finally figured out the purpose of your life. Your legacy inspired me to write this book, and hopefully, it will inspire and help other victims of abuse. More than any other chapter in this book, your tragic story of abuse and neglect needs to be told so everyone knows your life did have value and did have meaning.

You often said, "Someday when I die, I am going to see God and be happy with Him in Heaven." Whenever you made that announcement, you always smiled and your eyes lit up like a Christmas tree. It was as if dying was the greatest thing you had to look forward to. Sadly, for you, it probably was, but none of us knew the "someday" you were speaking of would happen so soon. I miss you, and I hope and pray one day I will see you happy in Heaven.

CONTENTS

PREFACE

MY FAVORITE QUOTE by Mark Twain is: "The two most important days in your life are the day you are born and the day you find out why."

This is my why.

As a newspaper journalist, I interviewed subject-matter professionals and passionately wrote about several serious social issues plaguing our country—teen pregnancies, abortions, sexually transmitted diseases, alcohol and substance abuse prevention, identity theft, depression, suicide prevention, and especially spouse and child abuse prevention.

Meanwhile, this book has been a project in waiting—my own true story as a survivor of a traumatic and abusive childhood.

After making it through my childhood, I felt like I could survive anything. No matter what happened to me in my adult life, I knew the worst part of my life was over.

Dr. Phil McGraw often says on his TV show that whenever children are abused or witness spousal abuse, "It changes them. It changes who they are and who they become." I know from experience that Dr. Phil is right.

Growing up in a dysfunctional home where spouse and child abuse reigned changed me and all eleven of my siblings. We will never know what we might have become if we had been raised in a loving home instead of a dysfunctional one, but I am very proud of what we have been able to do with our lives and careers in spite of it.

We became well-educated, contributing members of society, while statistics show we would have been far more likely to become alcoholics, drug addicts, or criminals. Thankfully, we were able to avoid becoming part of those statistics. That does not mean, however, that no damage was done. For me, it manifested itself in other ways—some negative, others positive. I spent much of my adult life trying to repair the damage done to me as a child. I am sure my siblings did the same, each in their own way.

TENDENCY TO OVERPROTECT MY OWN CHILDREN

Because I was not protected enough when I was a child, I overprotected my children. Whenever anything went wrong, I immediately ran to their rescue and fixed everything for them. Because I always came to my sons' rescue, they became too dependent on me as adults. It prevented them from paying consequences for their own bad choices, learning from their mistakes, and becoming all they could be. That is not good either.

Most of the time, protecting our children is the right thing to do. However, I know now that it is also necessary to let children pay some consequences for making poor decisions. When we are adults, the consequences for bad decisions become so much more serious and painful, so it is better to learn some of those lessons while we are still young.

Feeling the repercussions for our own actions is part of the learning and growing process that everyone must go through to become responsible, independent adults. I wish I knew this before my sons were born. Once set, the habit of overprotecting is a difficult mold to break.

With better parenting, my sons might have accomplished so much more because they are both highly intelligent. Unfortunately, they grew up without an involved father present during the majority of their childhood, and I was so busy working and attending college (putting myself together) that I had little energy left to provide proper parenting. Even if I fully understood what proper parenting meant, I still was not able to "be there" as often as I should have.

Of course, I did the best I could under the circumstances, but by overprotecting my sons as children, I caused them to develop an unreasonable sense of entitlement and failed to teach them the importance of setting and pursuing worthwhile goals. Even now, as adults, my sons still expect me to swoop in and fix their problems. Looking at the large number of adult children who still live at home, I believe many parents from my generation did the same thing.

Regardless of what I have been able to do with my life in spite of my child abuse, it definitely affected the way I raised my children. I did not physically abuse my children, but the complete lack of strong discipline was not good either.

ONLY MADE ME STRONGER

While I was in my third year of college as a full-time day student at the University of Puget Sound (UPS) in Tacoma,

Washington, my first husband of twelve years unexpectedly filed for a divorce. I had just finished supporting him through college when he took all the money out of our bank account.

As a single parent, I believed it now became even more important for me to remain in college and graduate so I could make a decent living for myself and my two sons, who were five and ten years old at the time. It was not easy, but many wonderful people came into my life when I needed them most, including my adviser at UPS, Rosemary Van Arsdel.

Rosemary said that I was a good student and she wanted to help me remain in college. She arranged for me to get some tuition money back from an emergency university fund, and she even offered to give me some "bread and milk" money out of her own pocket if I needed it. I felt the university supported me 150 percent. I also got another scholarship and three part-time jobs, so I managed to make house, car, and college payments all at the same time.

Friends told me it would be impossible for me to keep my house and stay in college as a single parent. I always liked it when someone told me I would not be able to accomplish something because that always made me all the more determined to do it.

One sunny afternoon when I was on my deck working on a college art project, my neighbor, whom I'll call Darcy, hollered over her fence and asked if she could come for a visit. That was one visit I will never forget because the conversation came as a huge surprise.

"You know, I envy you," she said.

"What? Why in the world would you envy me?" I asked. "I don't even know where my next meal is coming from ... and you are young and pretty, and you have a husband and two cute kids and no financial worries. So why would you envy me?"

"Because you are strong like a rock," Darcy said. "No matter what happens, you keep putting one foot in front of the other. I wish I was strong as a rock like you, but if I were in your shoes, I would shatter like glass."

At the time Darcy said that, I didn't feel very strong, but she saw something in me and in herself that I did not yet see.

A few years later, Darcy's self-analysis was put to the test when her cheating husband suddenly filed for divorce and ran off with another woman. By that time, I had graduated from UPS and had a full-time job. Now Darcy was attending college at Pacific Lutheran University, located within walking distance of our homes, making us alumni rivals. The only difference between her situation and the one I had a few years earlier was that she did not have the financial stress I had, and she did not have to get a job. In fact, the first thing Darcy did was to go out and buy a brand-new car, something I could never have done.

At first, Darcy appeared to be doing okay. After she started dating, however, her former husband was able to gain custody of her children with claims of child neglect. That's when Darcy's mental health quickly went downhill, and she soon became suicidal. Unfortunately, she even attempted to jump from the Tacoma Narrows Bridge. After she was rescued, she spent a few months in a psychiatric ward at Western State Hospital. Darcy was highly intelligent, and she told me how she was able to fool the doctors into releasing her early. I knew that my other neighbors and I needed to keep a close watch on her because she was not yet stable.

The last time I saw Darcy she came over to use my telephone because her phone was out of service. Nobody had cell phones yet. As Darcy was leaving, she stood at the top of my stairs staring in a strange way at my lighted Christmas tree with her big, sad, brown eyes. Her gaze reminded me of how a person might look at something for the very last time—the way you would look at something you might never see again.

I asked Darcy if she had her tree up yet, and she said she saw no purpose in putting a tree up since she no longer had her children. I then asked if she would be able to see them for Christmas.

"No," Darcy said. "The only way I would get a chance to see my children for Christmas is if I were dead, and they would get to come to my funeral."

Her statement bothered me, so the next day I went over to see her, just as she was leaving for Canada to spend the holidays with her rich, alcoholic mother. Unfortunately, that was probably the worst place she could have gone. I noticed that whenever her mother came for a visit, Darcy got worse, not better.

A few days later, I received the awful news that Darcy had died at the young age of thirty-six. I heard she ran out of her mother's home without a coat or shoes and did not take her diabetic medication with her. By the time she was found, she went into a diabetic coma and had a cardiac arrest. I do not know what was written on her death certificate, but I have no doubt the true cause of Darcy's death was suicide.

I previously stopped Darcy from committing suicide once before, and I sometimes wonder if she would still be alive if I could have prevented her from going to Canada that Christmas. Somehow, I don't think it would have done any good.

I kept thinking about that conversation Darcy had with me on my deck a few years earlier when she appeared to have a much happier life, free of worries. Now it made sense when she said she envied me at the time. Darcy knew her own limitations and vulnerabilities. She knew I had what it takes to get through difficult times in life, but if she were in the same situation, she would "shatter like glass."

If my abusive childhood is what made me "strong like a rock," perhaps that might be the one good thing that came of it.

MY STORY OF SURVIVAL

According to national child abuse statistics from the Centers for Disease Control and Prevention and the Adverse Childhood Experiences (ACE) study, "The United States has one of the worst records of child abuse among industrialized nations—losing on average between four and seven children every day to child abuse and neglect." Even worse, this national data is likely to underestimate the number of children who die from maltreatment. This report states, "It is estimated that between 50 to 60 percent of child fatalities due to maltreatment are not recorded as such on death certificates."

I know this is true in my family's case. Two of my sisters died without medical treatment, but parental neglect was not properly stated on their death certificates. Further, I nearly became part of those statistics myself.

In spite of my beginnings, I not only survived—I thrived. By writing this book, I hope I can inspire others to find the spirit and determination to do the same. No matter how many obstacles we have to overcome, we can survive and must never give up hope for a better life.

I was the sixth born from a family of fourteen children—seven girls and seven boys, no twins. I am mostly writing about my own experiences and observations, with the exception of some quotes seven of my siblings gave me permission to include.

I am certain most of my brothers and sisters have many of their own painful stories of survival. Some of them said it would be too difficult to revisit their childhood trauma, so they have chosen to suppress it instead—leaving the past in the past. I have discovered, however, that people must often go backward before they can go forward.

Imagine a vehicle stuck in the snow or mud. The driver goes back and forth until the vehicle is no longer stuck and lurches forward. People are often like that. Sometimes, to avoid getting stuck, it is important to look back to see where we have been. Chances are we can then find a much smoother road ahead.

Nonetheless, everyone must deal with painful experiences in their own way. My way is to dig it up by the roots. The more I do that, the prouder I am of myself for having survived all that I have. I feel that writing my story is therapeutic, but that is not the only reason I decided to share my story of survival with the world. I want others who might have similar struggles to know that difficult times can change for the better. We cannot control our beginnings, but we can create new and better endings.

To give readers a better understanding of my story, I am including a chapter of general background information on each of my parents.

They owned three different farms in Minnesota during their marriage, but most of us grew up near the small town of Glenwood, where I started first grade and graduated from high school in the same school building.

Our family attended the Sacred Heart Catholic Church every Sunday, went to confession once every six weeks, and prayed the rosary on our knees every night during the forty days of Lent. Meanwhile, back on the farm, we endured a very dysfunctional and abusive home environment on a regular basis. Most of the time, my father called my mother the "Old Lady," and my mother called my father the "Old Man." In this book, I will simply refer to them as Ma and Pa. No last names will be used.

All of my stories are true. I am using real first names of those who are now deceased, but I changed the names of most of my living siblings to protect the identity of those who might wish to remain anonymous unless given permission to use their real first name. At the time of this writing, six of us are now in our seventies, five are in their sixties, and one is still in his fifties.

I considered referring to my siblings as Child One through Child Fourteen. A friend said, "Oh, but that sounds so clinical." My first response was, "Good. That is precisely the point." I believe most of us felt like we were just numbers, at least in Pa's eyes—not children to be loved and cared for, but numbers of free farmhands to do all the chores, field work, and harvesting that needed to be done.

Direct quotes will be used—sometimes because the words were repeated so often I remember exactly what was said, and other times because it was such a horrific experience the words have been embedded in my brain forever. I will also use some quotes directly from Pa's handwritten autobiography, which he finished writing just two weeks before he died. He told Ma to give it to me because he recognized me as the writer in the family, even though I was not yet working as a professional newspaper reporter. I was already majoring in English-writing (journalism).

I did not know what Pa expected me to do with his

autobiography, but I typed it exactly as he had written it, only correcting misspelled words. I then sent out copies to my siblings who had email addresses and sent hard copies to the rest. A few of my siblings returned Pa's manuscript unopened because their hatred still ran so deep they did not want to know what he had to say.

I also heard a few siblings did not believe Pa actually wrote some of the things he did, especially that he "wished he could give (us) all back," but I still have Pa's handwritten copy to prove he wrote every word. Of course, the experiences of us older children compared to the younger children vary, because we each saw and heard different things at various stages of Pa's life. A few siblings might be in denial about some things, but I am writing what I know from what I experienced.

Ma often said terrible things to us kids about Pa, and Pa often said terrible things to us about Ma. I felt they used us children as weapons to punish each other. I cannot speak for my siblings, but all of the mean, nasty things my parents said about each other only gave me a worse opinion of both of them. Without question, Pa was by far the more abusive— at least, the more physically abusive, and the one we feared most.

By the time Pa passed away, Ma and Pa had been married forty-one years, but that marriage was a disaster from the start. At best, it was a love-hate relationship. They never should have been married, much less have fourteen children. I never saw Ma and Pa hug or kiss, and I never saw a hint of the kind of love and respect that normal, healthy, happily married couples show toward one another. The firstborn, Tom, said he remembered seeing our parents hug and kiss, but any sign of romance had disappeared by the time I was born. In fact, I saw and heard only the opposite. I saw Pa physically beat Ma several times, and some of those times she must have been pregnant when he did it. After all, Ma was pregnant most of the time. I cannot help but wonder if one of Pa's beatings might have been the cause of one of Ma's miscarriages and/or their stillborn child. If all of Ma's pregnancies had resulted in live births, there would have been seventeen of us.

My parents were both nonsmokers. As a child, I never knew anyone who used drugs or smoked pot. I never saw Ma or Pa drink alcohol, beer, or wine—not once. They never bought it, and it was never in the house. I often thought it might have been better if Pa had been an alcoholic—then I could have blamed his abusive behavior on the alcohol. Instead, Pa was sober when he abused us, so I always knew he did it on purpose. However, I now believe Pa must have been suffering from some form of mental illness, since no well-adjusted person could have possibly done some of the things he did. Mental illness just wasn't talked about much in those days. Regardless, Ma and Pa were both adult children of alcoholic fathers, and, no doubt, that affected how both of them behaved in some very negative ways. One thing I know for sure from my own experience is that outside appearances can be very deceiving.

My mother, Madeline, age two years, 1918
(She was wearing old-fashioned button-up shoes.)

MY MOTHER'S HISTORY

MADELINE, the oldest of nine children, was born on October 15, 1916, in Warroad, Minnesota. She passed away from cancer at age ninety-three on November 6, 2009, at Frazee Care Center in Frazee, Minnesota. Her tombstone marker had been engraved years earlier with the first two digits of the year of her death as "19," so it had to be corrected.

Ma often said, "My sixties and seventies were the best years of my life." Not surprising. It was the first time in many years she was no longer pregnant, and after Pa passed away, she no longer had to endure spousal abuse. God gave Ma nearly twenty-nine more years to enjoy life again as a free woman.

Ma lived alone at a lake home in Maine, Minnesota, near Phelps Mill, from the age of sixty-four (when Pa passed away) until she was eighty-eight. She spent the last five years of her life in a nursing home—about five years at the Battle Lake Good Samaritan Home and two months at the Frazee Care Center in Frazee, Minnesota. Ma felt much more at peace after she moved to the Frazee Care Center because Tom, her firstborn son, lived in Frazee, so he could stop in during lunch to see how she was doing.

Ma's mother, Grandma Marian, grew up in an orphanage, and at age seventeen, she married RB, a commercial fisherman and mink rancher. Ma was born in Warroad, Minnesota, and spent much of her time as a child on boats and beaches in an area known as the Lake of the Woods in northern Minnesota. She often talked about playing on sandy beaches and how hard she worked removing fish from nets. Ma also remembered how tight money was during the Great Depression, but she grew up in a loving home. She was definitely a "Daddy's girl."

THE PITCHFORK

The first five years of my life, at our Braham farmhouse, we were dependent on an old windmill to generate electricity, and whenever we lost power, all the lights would go off. However, we were never left in the dark for long because Ma always lit beeswax candles.

When I was three years old, Ma went to help Pa in the barn. When all the lights went out and it was too dark for her to see in the barn, Ma accidentally stepped on a pitchfork that had fallen on the barn floor with the tines facing up. When Ma came into the house limping, I saw blood dripping from one foot. Ma did not want to drip blood on the floor she had cleaned earlier that day, so she ordered me to bring her a towel. As much as I wanted to help, I felt like I was glued to the floor and couldn't move. Seeing all that blood petrified me, but Ma didn't understand. She was furious she had to get her own towel because she got blood on the clean floor.

That evening during supper, Pa blamed my older brothers for Ma stepping on the pitchfork.

"If you always put the pitchforks up against the barn wall with the tines facing out, this would have never happened," he said. "Then, even if the pitchfork falls over, the tines would be facing down instead of up and nobody would get hurt."

That was my first safety lesson, and I still remember what Pa told my older brothers every time I balance a garden hoe, shovel, or any other tool against a wall.

THE GROCERY LIST

When I was eleven years old, Grandma came to our farmhouse to help take care of me and my other brothers and sisters while Ma recovered from a miscarriage. When Grandma wrote a grocery list, I told her she would have to add some extra luxury grocery items we didn't really need.

"Why would I need to do that?" she asked.

"Because Pa buys only half the stuff on the list, so Ma always writes extra items she doesn't really need like ice cream, cake mix, and butter. Then he has more things he can cross out, and she's more likely to get the groceries she really needs."

"Oh, that's ridiculous," Grandma said. "Why on Earth would he do a thing like that?"

"He wants to feel like he's saving money, and he wants to prove to Ma that he's the boss in charge of all the money."

"Well, we'll see about that," Grandma said.

When Pa got home from the store, Grandma started

checking things on her list, and sure enough, Pa bought only half of the groceries. As soon as she discovered that, Grandma let loose with a very impressive Irish temper. After she read Pa the riot act, she made some demands of her own.

"Francis, you go right back to that store and get the rest of the items on this list," Grandma said. "You had all these children, and now you have a responsibility to feed them. I cannot cook for them with only half the things on this list."

Pa didn't say a word and did exactly as Grandma ordered. I was shocked. That was the first time I saw a woman have control over Pa. I decided right then and there that I wanted to be just like my grandma and have power over all the men in my life just like she did.

Ma said Grandma had red hair when she was young, so I figured there must be some magic in red hair. Therefore, I wanted to have red hair, too, but I didn't have hair color or the money to buy some, so I did the next best thing. I found some red food coloring and used that. The next day I proudly went to school with red hair.

"What's the name of your hair color?" a classmate asked. "I really like it, and I want to color my hair, too."

I would have been too embarrassed to admit I used food coloring, so I made up a name.

MA'S LIFE BEFORE PA

As I helped Grandma cut green beans from our garden and peel potatoes, she told me many stories about Ma's childhood.

Grandma said that, as their firstborn child, Ma was spoiled by her father, RB. He lavished a lot of attention on her, and whenever Ma threw temper tantrums, her dad always let her have her own way.

"It only got worse as she got older," Grandma said.

Ma only went through eighth grade in school, and she did not do well there. She was left-handed, and in those days, teachers punished students for being left-handed. They tried to force all children to be right-handed. Whenever teachers caught Ma printing with her left hand, they ruthlessly slapped her left hand with a long wooden ruler. Most likely, that is why she did not enjoy school and had no desire to continue her education.

Times were tough during Ma's childhood because the country was going through the Great Depression. After Ma left school, she worked for a few years as a waitress. On weekends, she often went to barn dances. Ma was a very beautiful woman, and at 110 pounds, 5 feet 7 inches tall, she always had plenty of dance partners waiting in line. She loved dancing, but I remember only about four times Pa took her to a dance throughout their entire forty-one-year marriage. I never saw Pa dance, but Ma still danced the polka until she was in her eighties.

DATING AND MARRIAGE

In Ma's day, very few young women were career minded. Most of them had no career ambition, other than becoming housewives and mothers. If young women were not married or engaged by eighteen, they started to worry about becoming old maids, and they often felt tremendous social pressure to get a ring on their finger.

Ma was twenty-three and Pa was twenty-seven when they married in June 1940, but Pa was not the man Ma intended to marry. He was just the one she got stuck with when she played a dating game that went terribly wrong.

Ma told me about Roy and Swede, two young men she dated before she met Pa. She said she fell deeply in love with Roy, and it sounded like he was pretty crazy about her, too. Unfortunately, Ma was feeling the pressure to get a ring on her finger, but Roy was not moving quickly enough in that direction. She got very excited when Roy wrote her a letter saying he had a special surprise to give her the next time he saw her. Ma was certain that it would be an engagement ring. To her disappointment, however, Roy gave her his high school ring instead. To Roy, that was a big deal—a symbol that Ma was his special girl and they were going steady. However, that was not good enough for her, and it made her very angry.

Shortly after that, Ma met Pa on a highway when he stopped to fix a flat tire on her friend's car. Her friend happened to be Pa's cousin. At that time, Roy was still Ma's steady beau, but when Pa asked her on a date, she saw it as an opportunity to make Roy jealous. She said she started dating Pa to put a fire under Roy's butt and get a marriage proposal out of him. Unfortunately, her dating game backfired.

Instead of becoming motivated to marry her, Roy felt terribly hurt and betrayed when Ma stepped out on him. She never heard from Roy again, and Ma was deeply heartbroken. She frequently talked about her previous beaus, and whenever she talked about Roy, her eyes sparkled and she had a radiant smile. I never saw that same look on her face when she was with Pa.

Shortly after Ma and Pa started dating, he was the one who proposed and offered her an engagement ring.

"I only accepted it because I thought Roy would try to win me back," she said. Unfortunately, that never happened. After losing her one true love, Ma said she felt she had no alternative but to remain engaged to Pa and go through with the wedding.

"It was the practical thing to do because at least he had a farm and could support me," she said.

Nonetheless, I believe Ma regretted her decision to marry Pa nearly every day of her life. That might explain some of the constant conflict she and Pa had. I do not believe Ma ever let go of her conflicted emotions over losing her one true love.

"I just wanted to have four children, not fourteen, but once I joined the Catholic Church, I did not have any say in the matter," Ma said. Before she married Pa, Ma was Presbyterian.

Ma and Pa were not allowed to get married in the Catholic Church because Ma was not yet a baptized Catholic. The bride and groom both had to be Catholic to be married in the sanctuary of the church. In those days, it could take five years to complete the required classes to convert to the Catholic religion, and Pa did not want to wait that long. That's why they got married in the parish rectory instead. Ma finally completed her Catechism studies and officially became a baptized Catholic shortly after her second son, Bernie, was born.

Oftentimes I found Ma sitting in a dark corner of the kitchen, sobbing. When I asked her what was wrong, she would say Pa did not really love her. Then she talked about how devastated she felt when she learned on her wedding night that he was not a virgin like she was.

"After he took my virginity away from me, he told me about another woman he had been with in Minneapolis," Ma said. "It was supposed to be the first time for both of us. He did not deserve to have a virgin. I wasted my virginity on him, and that was not fair."

I do not believe Ma ever forgave Pa for not being a virgin on their wedding night. She said she felt Pa had deceived her, and she agonized over it for many years. For Ma to assume that a twenty-seven-year-old man never had sex with any other woman was not realistic, at least not for my generation, but that is exactly what she expected.

"Whatever you do, it's very important for you to find a virgin man who never slept with another woman," Ma said. "If you find a virgin man, then you will have a loyal husband for life."

Because that was so important to Ma, she made me believe that it should be important to me, too. Therefore, I did find a virgin man, but that's why my first husband was younger than me. I was the first and only girlfriend my first husband had. All the other guys my age or older were no longer virgins, and they were proud of it. Now I know that getting married to a "virgin man" who had never "sowed his wild oats" was the worst advice I ever got from Ma, and one of the root causes of my divorce.

LIFE ON THE FARM

I asked Ma why she did not drive, especially since she did not have to take a written or behind-the-wheel test in those days. She said she drove the Hudson car once when Tom and Bernie were little boys, and somehow she backed it into a ditch and got stuck. A neighbor came along and pulled the car out of the ditch for her, but when Pa found out what happened, he forbade her to ever drive again.

Later, when I was about eight, Ma was once again fighting for her right to drive the car, and Pa finally agreed to let her try to take our car out for a practice drive. Unfortunately, Ma never even got out of the driveway. I was watching as she spun the tires in place, like a cartoon character running in place without going anywhere. The wheels kicked up so much dirt that they left a five-inch trench in the driveway. The car had to be a stick shift, and she must have had one foot on the gas and one foot on the brake or clutch all at the same time. I don't think cars had automatic transmissions yet.

"This proves it," Pa said, as he pointed to the evidence in the driveway. "You simply are not smart enough to learn how to drive, and you never will be."

Not long after that, Ma developed such bad eyesight that she might not have been able to pass an eye exam to drive a car, anyway. She eventually went blind in one eye.

Throughout my childhood, during cold Minnesota winters, I often watched Ma as she fed, changed, and bathed my younger siblings. She turned the oven on, opened the oven door, and put a small kitchen table over the oven door. Then she placed soft baby blankets on the table. That is how she kept the babies warm in winter months while giving them a bath. I could tell from the way she played "This Little Piggy Goes to Market" on their toes that she really loved her babies. They were like living dolls, and Ma was in her own little dreamland.

In the early part of their marriage, Ma was pretty high-spirited and often mouthed off to Pa, but after several years of enduring physical spousal abuse, she became just as afraid of him as we were. When Pa was in an extra bad mood because an animal was sick or something else went wrong, we kids would often run to hide, and Ma would sometimes hide with us.

Most of the time Ma did what she could to take care of us whenever we were sick. Unfortunately, Ma never had the emotional maturity, courage, and stability needed to protect us from harm. Sometimes she even used us, like shields, to protect herself. One example of this was the broken pitcher.

THE BROKEN PITCHER

One day in a fit of anger, Ma threw a plastic drinking pitcher across the floor and broke it. Pa was furious when he saw the broken pitcher and wanted to know who broke it. Ma was too afraid to tell him she did it. Instead she remained silent and watched as he lined all of us kids up and started spanking each one from oldest to youngest.

That was Pa's golden rule: If he did not know which kid did what, he spanked all of us so he could make sure he got the guilty one.

"If you admit you did it, I will not spank you," Pa said.

After seeing Pa whip the heck out of my older brothers and sisters, I was so scared by the time he got to me that I said I did it so I wouldn't get spanked. That was a big mistake because Pa lied. He whipped me twice as hard instead, and even that was not good enough.

"Now to learn your lesson, you need to put your snowsuit on and take this pitcher to the end of the field and throw it in the ditch," he said.

I was only six years old, and he expected me to walk two miles in a snow blizzard. When I was putting my snowsuit on, Ma came to my room to see me.

"I'm sorry, Barbie, but if I told him I did it, he would have beat me twice as hard," she said.

I thought Ma might be right, but I still did not understand how she could let me take the punishment for what she did.

When I saw how deep the snowbanks were, I knew it would be impossible to walk those two miles. With every step I took, I sank down into deep snow, and I soon got so cold I knew I would never make it all the way there and back alive. So I cheated and threw the broken pitcher somewhere else, hoping Pa would never find it. With acres and acres of land, what were the chances?

As it turned out, the chances were extremely good. The next spring I could hardly believe it when Pa found the broken pitcher. He was furious that I took it only one mile instead of two, so he made me take it the rest of the way, but at least it was a lot easier to walk that far after the snow had melted.

MA'S POSITIVE CHARACTERISTICS

Some of Ma's most positive characteristics were her love of music, dancing, and flowers. Without fail, Ma always planted flowers in front of our house every summer.

At our Braham farm, we had lilac bushes a few feet from our dining room windows. When the lilacs were in bloom on warm summer days, Ma cut a bouquet to put on our dining room table and opened the windows. I remember the strong, sweet fragrance of the lilacs that filled the Braham farmhouse.

Ma often talked about a beautiful rose bush she once had in the front yard, too, but Pa backed over it with a tractor, and it never bloomed again.

"He destroyed that rose bush on purpose just to be mean, because he knew how much I loved it," she said.

At our Glenwood farmhouse, Ma mostly planted bachelor's buttons, gladiolas, zinnias, and morning glories. No matter how awful life got, she always took time to plant, care for, and smell her flowers.

Ma also enjoyed singing her favorite songs and telling us bedtime stories. Oftentimes, she told us spooky bedtime stories from her own childhood.

ADVICE FROM MA

I believe the best advice Ma gave me was:

- Get a good education so you can get a good enough job to support yourself.

- Get a driver's license to maintain your independence.

- Keep money in your own secret bank account so you can leave if a man ever hits you.

"Do not wait for a man to hit you a second time," Ma said. "If a man hits you once, he will hit you again, and the next time he will hit you much harder."

I believe Ma gave the girls in the family this advice because she wanted us to have better lives than she did. I know she felt trapped in her marriage to Pa, and she did not want us to experience a similar fate.

I think the best advice Ma gave to the boys in the family probably was to "join the military." She greatly admired military drill instructors and said they were like miracle workers.

"I tried for several years to teach your brothers how to fold clothes and make beds, and finally I just gave up," Ma said. "I don't know how drill instructors do it, but after just a short time in boot camp, they taught your brothers how to make beds, fold socks, and hang up shirts. That is why all young men ought to join the military. It's the best way for them to become domesticated enough for any woman to put up with them."

MA'S FUNERAL

Several times over the last twenty years before Ma passed away, I rushed home because I thought she was on her deathbed. Shortly after I got there, however, she would get up, take her oxygen mask off, and start rocking back and forth in her rocking chair as if nothing happened.

"Ma, I thought you were dying, but you seem fine to me," I said.

"Oh, sometimes I just have to fake it to get you kids to come home to visit me," she said.

I was on my way back to Minnesota on a thirty-six-hour Amtrak train ride when Ma passed away two hours before I got there. Ma told me many times that when she passed away, she wanted all twelve of us children to attend her funeral. She got her wish. We came from eight states, and we were all there. Many grandchildren and great-grandchildren attended as well.

I met a man on the Amtrak who said he had taken the train home to attend his mother's funeral on 9/11.

"Out of ten children, I was the only one who made it home for my mother's funeral, because my other nine brothers and sisters were on airplanes that were grounded," he said. "I've been traveling by train ever since."

Shortly before my mother passed away at age ninety-three, I joked with her on the telephone.

"A world champion speaker in Toastmasters International gave a speech and said, 'When we die, the number of people who will attend our funeral will largely depend on the weather that day,'" I told her. "So if you want to make sure all twelve of us children attend your funeral, you better not die during a Minnesota snow blizzard."

"Don't worry," she replied. "I'll be sure to die on a good-weather day so none of you have an excuse not to attend."

Ma kept her promise, because it was a good-weather day, and all twelve of her living children, ages fifty to sixty-eight at the time, attended her funeral. I know that meant a lot to her. If there's such a thing as a happy funeral, Ma had one.

When we were putting Ma to rest, however, one thing happened during the graveyard ceremony that might have disappointed her. As each of us five surviving daughters stood in order of age, oldest to youngest, by Ma's grave, the Catholic priest handed Pat the aspergillum (holy water shaker) for her to sprinkle holy water on Ma's casket and pass it down for each of us to do the same. When it came to Ann's turn, she refused to sprinkle holy water on Ma's casket and immediately passed it down to the youngest daughter, Missy, instead. I wondered if Ann still had ill feelings toward Ma.

Before Ma passed away, she expected each of us children to remember her with a gift or a phone call on Mother's Day and her birthday. Whenever I called her, Ma would list all of the children who were in her doghouse because they failed to remember her. I often thought she must have written them down, and after Ma passed away, I discovered I was right. When I went through her address book to get phone numbers of friends and relatives to notify, I found a list of all of the children who were in her doghouse for the last several years.

Ma had a beautiful casket with decorative roses on the sides, and her oldest daughter, Pat, sang "How Great Thou Art," one of Ma's favorite church hymns. Matt was the only sibling allowed to give a eulogy. Initially, the Catholic priest said the Mass was enough and no eulogy would be allowed. That's what I don't like about Catholic funerals. They usually don't allow anyone to give a eulogy, and I think that's awful. Allowing family members and friends to give a eulogy at a funeral is really part of the healing process, and it's more for the living than the dead.

Finally, the priest agreed to make an exception and allow

my brother Matt to give a eulogy before the Mass started, but only on the condition he could see a written copy beforehand that he would or would not approve. Matt said the priest crossed out some statements.

"You cannot say that your mother went to Heaven because we do not know that for sure," the priest said.

Matt was upset over some of the priest's comments, and when he gave Ma's eulogy, he ignored some of the guidance he received from the priest and gave his original comments without even looking at his script. Below is a copy of the eulogy Matt gave for our mother.

Eulogy

Welcome to all family members, friends, and neighbors of (our mother). Mom's friends called her Maggie. Maggie grew up in Warroad, Minnesota, and she was the oldest of nine children. Maggie's dad and brothers were fishermen. Maggie loved to fish.

Some time ago while visiting Maggie, I asked her, "Mom, do you know the way to Heaven?" She said, "Of course I do. It is through Jesus Christ, my Lord and Savior."

One of Jesus's disciples also asked this question, saying, "Master, how do we get to Heaven?" Jesus answered saying, "I am the way, the truth, and the light. No man comes to the Father but through me."

"For God so loved the world that He gave His only begotten Son, that whoever believes in Him shall not perish, but have eternal life."

The departing words of Jesus to his disciples were, "I go to prepare a place for you, so that where I am, you may be also."

Maggie had a loving and forgiving heart. God knows our heart, and God knows our true intent. As for forgiveness, Jesus put it in the middle of the Lord's Prayer. After we ask God to forgive us our trespasses, it says: "As we forgive those who trespass against us."

Can we truly believe God will forgive us if we are unwilling to forgive one another? I think not.

As most of you know, Maggie loved people. The one thing Maggie loved most was to have company. She would clean her house and bake the best food she had available for the company. Maggie would freely give the best she had.

She also had an extensive prayer life. Maggie told me that she would pray for every member of her family every day. When she prayed, she would shut off the TV and radio, then get down on her knees, fold her hands, bow her head, and pray to Almighty God.

Maggie would also pray for her friends as they had needs. She was on a prayer chain, and she would pray for anyone in need of prayer. Maggie believed in the power of prayer, and I believe we are all better off because of Maggie's prayers. I know I am.

Maggie has made many friends over the past ninety-three years, many of whom have gone on before her. Maggie said something that surprised me about her friends. She said, "I have the best friends in the world.

God doesn't make them any better."

Maggie was no saint. She told me she had some regrets. I know some of her regrets involved the loss of her two daughters. Regrets are simply mistakes we make while going through life—those times when we say, "If only I could have a do-over, I would have done it differently." The good news is that God forgives confessed mistakes. I didn't come here to say good-bye to Mom but to remember all the good she did in her life and to say, "See you later, Mom!"

Ma and Pa on their wedding day June 3, 1940, in the church rectory of St. Mary's Catholic Church in Warroad, Minnesota.

MY FATHER'S HISTORY

MY FATHER, Francis, the oldest of three boys, weighed twelve pounds at birth on August 12, 1912, in Lisbon, North Dakota. After receiving about sixty bee stings, Pa passed away from a heart attack at the age of sixty-eight on April 18, 1981, at his lake home in Maine, Minnesota.

His mother, Daryl, was a nurse, and his father, Frank, was a farmer in Wisconsin. Pa's father was also a politician. He served as mayor of his local town and had a county board position, so he was gone quite often.

In spite of Pa's hot, uncontrollable temper, he was no dummy. Pa often bragged that he was so smart he got to skip a grade, but he only went through eighth grade. That's about as far as most kids went in school in those days.

According to Pa's autobiography, his father was "not easy to live with," so his mother frequently left his father. However, he gave no reasons why. He wrote that his father "scolded" his mother for leaving; that's all. He never mentioned physical violence. In fact, it appears that Pa got off easy when he was a kid. He never got spanked for shooting a hole in the floor of their living room or for setting some curtains on fire. Instead of yelling at him for not working hard enough (as Pa did with his own children), Pa's father complimented him for doing such a good job of milking cows. When Pa was a kid, he was taken to a hospital when he got pneumonia, but he failed to do the same thing for his own children. His parents even presented him with a new tricycle when he got well. It appears our Pa had an easy and happy childhood, compared to ours.

Pa owned three farms before he retired. The first five years of my life, we had a 200-acre farm near Braham, Minnesota, and from age five until I graduated from high school, we had a 400-acre farm near Glenwood, Minnesota. After Pa sold the Glenwood farm, he bought another 200-acre farm in Dalton, Minnesota.

I cannot speak for all of my siblings, but most of us did not love Pa. I can remember feeling only two things—fear and hate. He had a boiling-hot temper and ruled with an iron fist. What he called discipline was actually child abuse in the first degree. That's why we called him the Old Man, but for this book, I simply call him Pa.

PA'S BROTHERS

Pa had two younger brothers—Bernie and Mark.

Uncle Bernie flew airplanes in World War II, and after the war, he bought his own small airplanes that could seat two to four passengers, counting the pilot. Once he had a pontoon airplane so he could take off and land on water, but most of the time he flew underwing airplanes. When we lived in Braham, Minnesota, he flew his airplane to the farm and landed on a dirt road in the field. During his visit, we got a downpour of rain, and the dirt road got too muddy for takeoff. Therefore, they had to push his airplane to a gravel road and block off a section big enough for him to take off from there.

When we lived in Glenwood, Minnesota, it was much easier for Uncle Bernie to fly out for a visit because our farm was only about a half mile from the local municipal airport. Most of the local pilots would just fly normally, but our Uncle Bernie was not a "normal" pilot. During the war, he learned to dodge bullets, so he did not fly like other local pilots. Instead, when Uncle Bernie came to visit, he always got our attention by flying straight up, straight down, or by doing some loop-de-loops and other tricks in the sky.

When we were working in the fields and saw a plane doing tricks above us, we immediately knew only one pilot flew like that—our Uncle Bernie. So we dropped our pitchforks and beat feet to the airport, yelling, "Uncle Bernie's here! Uncle Bernie's here!" On one of his visits, he decided to give all of us kids an airplane ride, two at a time. I don't remember having a choice in the matter, but at five I had my first airplane ride with my "crazy" Uncle Bernie. It's no wonder I fear flying to this day, because he scared the hell out of me, and I couldn't wait to get back down on the ground.

Pa's youngest brother, Mark, was a wealthy businessman, but he passed away at twenty-eight from carbon monoxide poisoning when his vehicle got stuck in a snow blizzard. At the time of Uncle Mark's death, he owned some expensive business suits, and he had one business suit in particular that my Pa and Uncle Bernie both wanted to have. Bernie was married to a spunky woman named Kay. To their surprise, when Kay saw them fighting over their dead brother's suit, she grabbed it away from both of them and threw it in the fireplace.

Pa never served in the military. To be exempt from being drafted during World War II, Pa bought a farm with inheritance money he got from his grandmother, and he got married.

Pa got a lot of exercise when he was farming. After he retired, he continued to eat the same amount of food. For the first time in his life, he put on excess weight because he was no longer burning off the calories. A few weeks before Pa's fatal heart attack, Ma asked him to get a new suit because his old suit no longer fit him, and she was so glad he did.

"Otherwise, I would not have had anything to bury him in," she said.

THE MOTORCYCLE ACCIDENT

Many times I asked myself, "Whatever made Pa so angry and abusive in the first place?" He did not smoke or drink. I never saw him have a single glass of alcohol, wine, or beer, so his explosive temper could not be blamed on that.

After reading through Pa's autobiography, I came to a few conclusions. First, it was obvious that he had difficulty feeling and expressing emotions. His script was nearly void of normal human emotions. I would expect the deaths of his youngest brother, mother, grandmother, and two daughters would have filled his heart with a tremendous feeling of loss and sadness. Instead, Pa wrote about them as if he were giving the six o'clock news.

Second, I believe Pa lived with a deep sense of guilt over

his mother's death because he knew he was to blame. In fact, in today's world, Pa most likely would have been charged with negligent homicide.

It was June 15, 1936. Pa was twenty-four when he decided to ride his motorcycle from Minnesota to visit his brother Bernie in California. Pa's mother, Daryl, a nurse in Minneapolis, took a vacation to go with him. Pa said it would be too difficult for his mother to ride in the sidecar attached to his motorcycle for such a long trip. However, they decided that if it became too difficult, Pa would stop at a bus depot so she could take a bus the rest of the way. They had not traveled far when they came to some road construction in North Dakota. A flagman stopped them and told Pa not to drive on the oiled side of the road because it was dangerously slick. He was told that whenever there was oncoming traffic, however, he should carefully move over just long enough for other vehicles to pass.

The first time Pa moved over to the oiled side of the road, he slowed down and had no problem. Unfortunately, that gave him a false sense of his ability to keep his motorcycle under control. The next time Pa had to move over to the oiled side of the road, he was overly confident, was going too fast, and failed to use enough caution. This time, as soon as his motorcycle wheels touched the oil, the motorcycle spun out of control, smashing against the embankment so hard it broke the sidecar and ejected his mother like a rag doll. She was not wearing a helmet, and her head hit the pavement so hard that she did not even make it to the hospital. She was pronounced dead at the scene.

If Pa had used enough caution, he could have prevented his forty-six-year-old mother's untimely death, and nobody knew that better than he did. Pa lived with that guilt for the rest of his life, which might have been one reason he was such an angry person. He may have been angry at himself, but he just took his anger out on everyone around him—especially his wife and children.

A few years before the motorcycle accident that killed his mother, Pa wrote about a motorcycle race he and a friend had on an abandoned airstrip. Without motorcycle helmets or protective leathers, they raced at speeds of more than 100 miles per hour. If you consider the kind of motorcycles made in the 1930s, it would have been a very dangerous and reckless thing to do. Even riding that fast on today's motorcycles would be risky. Based on these previous behavior patterns of a young man who took high risks and was overly confident and cocky, in the very least, Pa was most likely guilty of negligent homicide.

When I was twelve, Pa bought a pink Indian motorcycle from a Minneapolis pawn shop for $100 and gave it to my older brothers, Tom and Bernie, who were seventeen and sixteen. The first thing they did was paint it Indian red.

One day at the dinner table, Pa bragged how he could balance his motorcycle well enough at a high speed that he could let go of the handlebars and stand straight up on the seat. He could tell from the looks on our faces that we did not believe him. Then Pa said, "In fact, I bet I could still do it, and I will prove it to you." He then told us kids to stand out in the yard and watch. He said he would take the motorcycle down the highway, get it up to the right speed, and when he passed our farmhouse, he would be standing straight up on the seat with his arms out. Amazingly, he actually did it, and we kids who were watching were rather impressed that Pa could do such a neat trick. Pa was forty-six at the time.

Now, looking back as an adult, I realize it was an irresponsible and immature thing for him to take such a high risk when he had more than a dozen children and a large farm to operate. He was not even wearing a motorcycle helmet or leather pants.

SANDY ACRES

Farming pretty much engulfed Pa's entire life. Once I saw Pa standing at the end of our 100-foot-long garden with his hands on his hips as he gazed over his fields of oats and corn. It appeared that he was truly proud of his farm, and he had a right to be because Pa was a highly successful farmer.

When Pa bought our farm in Glenwood, the soil was so bad for growing crops that some neighbors called it Sandy Acres, and they did not believe Pa could make a go of it. However, he knew what kind of manure and fertilizer to use and soon turned Sandy Acres into rich, black soil. Our corn crop was growing along one side of a main highway that led to the Twin Cities, and a neighbor's corn crop was on the other side. Our corn crop was usually twice as high as the neighbor's.

That was not by accident, either. Pa spent many hours reading and studying various farming magazines. He even made deals with corn seed companies to get his corn seed at reduced prices in exchange for posting advertising signs next to his impressive corn crops.

Within a very short time, Pa paid off the farm and had 500 pigs, 100 head of cattle, 30 cows, 5 tractors, and a big truck. He also built a couple pig houses, a two-car garage, and a machine shed, and he doubled the size of the barn. Pa had a name for each of his cows and kept records on how much milk and butterfat each cow produced, so I know Pa loved farming.

Pa could fix just about any piece of machinery that broke down. In fact, I grew up with the expectation that all men could fix nearly anything that broke. Pa and my seven brothers did. They could all fix just about anything. To my surprise, I later learned men are not born with those skills.

Pa was involved in the National Farmers Organization (NFO) and served for several years as president of the Pope County NFO—an organization of farmers who fought for fair prices for milk, cream, and produce such as wheat, oats, and corn. As the leader in the local NFO, Pa accumulated many anonymous enemies. To this day, I still suspect that some of those enemies were responsible for setting his farm on fire on September 26, 1967.

THE FIRE

I had already graduated from high school and was living in St. Paul, Minnesota, when I first learned about the fire while watching the news on TV. The local fire department was able to get there in time to save the house and prevent the outside gas tank from exploding, but my parents lost many buildings and animals. My brother Buzz was there, and this is what he wrote about it:

> When I was fifteen, we suddenly woke up at
> 4:30 a.m. to the dreaded word "fire." The fifty-
> five-gallon drums of gas that had been filled the
> day before had been spread between the buildings,
> so there were six-foot flames on bare ground. The

barns, granaries, and machine shed went up in a
huge fire. Thousands of bales of hay and straw,
thousands of bushels of oats, and about 100 pigs
were toasted. The cattle got out, but all of our
hard work went up in smoke. We were defeated.

Ma said she first discovered the fire when she got up during the night to fix a bottle for her infant grandson. She looked out the window and saw the fire when it first started, in a big straw pile.

"The reason the fire spread so quickly is because the arsonist spilled a trail of gasoline from the straw pile to all the buildings," Ma said. "They also doped the dog and locked him in the car."

Ma immediately alerted Pa to the fire and got all the kids out of bed. Ma then stood outside holding the baby and a metal case of important papers.

"I felt helpless as I stood there watching all the kids running into burning buildings to save whatever they could," she said. "Every time I saw them run into a burning building, I worried they might not come back out."

Pa drove his big truck out of the burning machine shed just before the roof collapsed, scraping and denting the side of it on his way out. My brothers Mark, Matt, and Buzz saved three of Pa's five tractors, but two of them burned up. One of the tractors that burned had $1,000 in cash in two $500 bills in a jar hidden in the tractor's toolbox. Amazingly, Pa later collected the ashes of the money, sent them to the Treasury Department, and got the $1,000 replaced.

Because Pa went through the Great Depression, he did not trust banks, so he divided his money up among several different banks. Pa also hid additional emergency money in glass jars and tin cans in various strange places on the farm.

I don't know how many buildings Pa managed to rebuild, but he rebuilt the barn in metal instead of wood. Ma said they took a terrible loss because they were underinsured.

PA'S VIEWS ON WOMEN

One of Pa's worst characteristics is that he did not show much, if any, respect for women. Often, when Ma was in her late stages of pregnancy, Pa mocked her by saying she looked like a fat sow about to deliver a litter of baby pigs. Worse yet, while we were all seated around the dinner table, boys on one side and girls on the other, Pa often announced, "Women are no good for nothing except to get married, have babies, and serve men!"

That comment made my sister Ann so angry that she was determined to prove Pa wrong. She was never going to become a baby machine or spend the rest of her life as a servant to any man. Instead, she became fiercely independent and defiant against the status quo. During her college years, she passionately participated in the Women's Rights Movement, stamped her letters with movement slogans, and never allowed herself to fall in love until after she earned her doctorate degree and had a high-paying job as a school principal.

Two older sisters and I once found the love letters Pa wrote to Ma during their courtship. We girls sat on a bed upstairs and read them, laughing our heads off because they were so dull—not romantic at all. Pa started his letters with "My Dearest" and ended them with "Love," but everything he wrote on the pages in between was about his pigs, cows, farm crops, and how much money he would make. Ma caught us reading her letters and took them away, but we had already read most of them, and they were all pretty much the same. It made me wonder if Pa ever really loved anyone.

PA'S HOBBIES

Pa did have a few hobbies, but work always came first. After church on Sunday afternoons, Ma and Pa sometimes enjoyed playing Whist card games with visiting neighbors. Pa also enjoyed ice fishing in winter months and fishing from rented rowboats during summer months, while most of us kids went swimming. Pa put on a bibbed one-piece swimsuit once and said he was going to go swimming, but after putting his toes in the water's edge, he said it was too cold and changed his mind. I suspected he never learned how to swim.

My older brothers had rifles for pheasant and duck hunting, but I never saw Pa go hunting with them. The only other hobby Pa had was raising honeybees. He had several rows of honeybee hives at the end of our 1,000-square-foot garden, and he made his own honey frames from scratch.

When the frames were full of honey, Pa heated up flat knives that he used to peel off the top thin layer of beeswax and then put four frames into a barrow-shaped extractor. We kids took turns cranking the handle that spun the inside basket around to make the honey fly out and drip down the inside of the outer barrow. We usually got enough honey every year to fill two cream cans. To prevent getting bee stings, Pa had a protective bee jumpsuit, a headpiece with a screen, and a smoke puffer. Yet, Pa often did not bother to use his protective gear and bragged that bee stings did not bother him. Once he purposely put a bee on his arm and invited it to sting him just to prove it.

LESSONS FROM PA

The most valuable lessons I learned from Pa were:

- A strong work ethic: Pa had a very strong work ethic, which he passed on to me and most of my brothers and sisters. In fact, some of us have such a strong work ethic that we have to schedule fun. We were trained that work always comes before pleasure.

- Discipline: Pa often crossed the line from discipline to abuse, but some of what we learned was beneficial to us in the long run. We children all became law-abiding citizens. We were trained to be courteous to senior citizens and to show respect for and obey everyone in positions of authority. No doubt, that helped us to stay out of trouble.

- How to control my mouth: Some of my brothers had their mouths washed out with bars of soap for cursing. Pa himself cursed plenty when he got angry, but we children were taught not to do the same.

- My Christian faith: Pa took us to church every Sunday, to Catechism every Saturday, and to confession once every six weeks. At the dinner table, he insisted we all say grace before eating. Both of my parents got on their knees to pray every morning and every night. I never heard either one of them ever pray for help to become better parents. Pa mostly prayed that if God would give him rain and a bumper crop, he would give more money to the church. Sometimes my parents fought all the way to church and all the way home again, so I often wondered why we bothered to attend church in the first place, but at least we did grow up knowing about the Holy Bible and the power of prayer. Once when my parents were having a terrible argument, I folded my hands and prayed, "Please God, make the old man shut up and go outside." To my surprise, right in the middle of a sentence, Pa instantly shut up and went outside. Wow! I felt like I received an immediate response to prayer.

When I read Pa's autobiography, I was surprised to see that he had written about a religious experience. This is what he wrote:

About 1960 or 1961, I had an experience that I would not trade for any price I can think of. We had a very dry summer, had finished harvest and threshing, and about August 16 or 18, I was mowing hay in the lower spots in the field west of the house. I was sad and disgusted over the poor season. I started thinking maybe there was no God. A short time later, I looked at the sky, and way over on the eastern horizon was a dark cloud. In all my life I had never seen a cloud in the east move west. Then I thought ... well, if that cloud comes up here and drops some rain, I'd believe there is a God. It would prove to me He knew my thoughts, and He could move the clouds at his will.

I kept on mowing, and my thoughts moved on to other things. Then maybe fifteen minutes later, I looked up and there was that cloud getting close, almost overhead, and I thought ... man, that's funny. I did not quit and go home to avoid a wetting. I just didn't believe that cloud would keep coming. But it did, and soon it was raining harder and harder, and I left for home. As I drove into the yard, I remembered my earlier thoughts that if that cloud came and dropped some rain, I'd believe in God. Then I said, "My God, I asked for this!"

I did not explain this to the family, but I had a lot to think about. That shower cloud had gone at least fifty miles in the wrong direction and dropped almost one inch of rain. Before that, and since, I've never seen a rain cloud go back west. Why did it happen the one time I wanted God to prove his existence? I've never doubted God's existence again. Very few people are privileged to get such a personal demonstration.

PA'S FUNERAL

Ten of the twelve living children attended Pa's funeral. My sister Pat and I did not. Two weeks before Pa passed away, my first husband left me and filed for divorce, so I was a single parent to my two young sons. Therefore, I was already dealing with another personal crisis, and I did not have enough money for airfare to fly from the West Coast to Minnesota to attend Pa's funeral. Even if I had the money to go, I probably still would not have attended. I did not have anyone to care for my sons while I was gone. But, honestly, Pa was already dead to me long before his physical passing.

When my mother phoned and told me that Pa had passed

away, I felt more relief than grief. Why? I knew that Pa could no longer abuse my mother or anyone else. I remember saying to myself, "Now Ma can live in peace." As coldhearted as it might sound, I did not grieve Pa's death any more than I would grieve a skunk getting run over on the road. I felt no loss. I had no feelings of love for him. I cannot ever remember feeling any love for Pa. I wish I could have, but all I could remember feeling toward Pa was fear—constant fear and hatred.

Ann said the only reason she attended Pa's funeral was "to make sure he was dead." Her therapist suggested she attend his funeral "to bury her hatred along with the dead." I heard reports from other family members that she openly laughed during Pa's funeral service. Mark's wife read Ann the riot act for being so blatantly disrespectful, but I was not surprised and couldn't really blame her.

Many years later, we celebrated Ma's ninetieth birthday in the church that's next to the graveyard where Pa is buried. Some of my sisters invited me to go with them to the church graveyard to visit his grave, but I declined because I had already been there with my granddaughter. A short time later, my sisters returned to the church laughing. They said Ann danced on his grave, and Rose spit on it.

My parents already had seven children when this photo was taken in 1948, but Katherine passed away at three months. I was age two, and I hated it when Pa cut my hair above my ears, but one of my earliest memories was when this photo was taken, and I still remember why I had a scowl on my face.

Left to right: Me, Rose, Pat, Bernie, and Tom.

EARLIEST MEMORIES

SEVERAL PEOPLE TOLD ME they can remember back only as far as when they were five years old, and it is impossible to have memories that go back farther. I disagree. I have some memories that go back to when I was two, and I can describe many details as if they happened yesterday.

I have read that how far back each person can remember largely depends on language skills, and Pa often bragged about how early we children acquired language skills. He said most of us could talk in complete sentences shortly after our first birthday.

I've also read that when people have had truly traumatic experiences, like I've had, they are much more likely to remember them because they usually leave a far greater imprint in the mind. This chapter includes some of those experiences, but not all of my childhood memories were bad ones. I do have some good memories, too. I just never felt safe until I graduated from high school and moved far away so Pa could never hurt me again.

Interestingly enough, Pa wrote in his autobiography:

> *The reason I was so hard on the kids is because the world is a difficult place, and I wanted my children to be tough enough to take whatever life had in store for them without having to lean on drugs or alcohol as a crutch.*

Perhaps in some ways he succeeded because all twelve of us living children are indeed strong and independent. Nonetheless, I had to question his motivation and overall objective. Far too often Pa's idea of discipline was nothing but child abuse in the first degree.

Timeline of Family Events

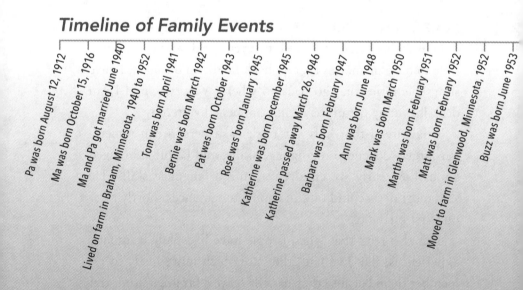

FAMILY PHOTO

As our family grew in size, every few years Pa had family photos taken at a professional photography studio. He always got several copies made to mail with annual Christmas cards to family members and friends. I never understood why he had those family photos taken. It was a rare indication he might have felt proud of his family. On the other hand, it could have been his way to "rub it in" to his only living brother, who was not able to have children.

One of those family photos was taken when my baby sister, Ann, was six months old. Because I am only fifteen months older than her, I must have been not quite two years old when that photo was taken. Yet, I still remember why I had a scowl on my face instead of a smile.

When we were ready to have our photo taken at the studio,

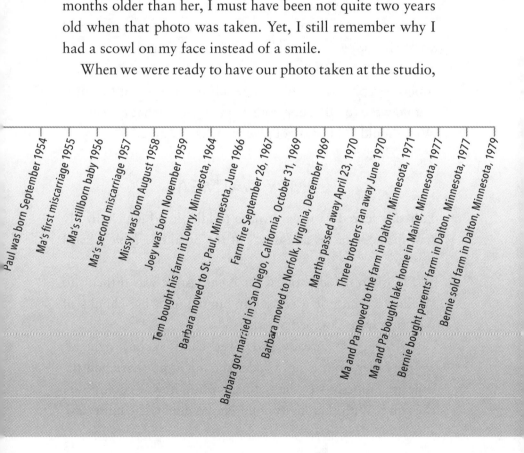

Paul was born September 1954
Ma's first miscarriage 1955
Ma's stillborn baby 1956
Ma's second miscarriage 1957
Missy was born August 1958
Joey was born November 1959
Tom bought his farm in Lowry, Minnesota, 1964
Barbara moved to St. Paul, Minnesota, June 1966
Farm fire September 26, 1967
Barbara got married in San Diego, California, October 31, 1969
Barbara moved to Norfolk, Virginia, December 1969
Martha passed away April 23, 1970
Three brothers ran away June 1970
Ma and Pa moved to the farm in Dalton, Minnesota, 1970
Ma and Pa bought lake home in Maine, Minnesota, 1971
Bernie bought parents' farm in Dalton, Minnesota, 1977
Bernie sold farm in Dalton, Minnesota, 1977
Bernie sold farm in Dalton, Minnesota, 1979

I was initially sitting on Ma's lap, and Ann was sitting on Pa's lap. I thought that was a fine arrangement because Pa always favored Ann over me. Just as I got ready to smile for the camera, the photographer changed it.

"The baby belongs on the mother's lap," he said, and he made Ma and Pa switch.

I was perfectly happy with the initial arrangement, but then I had to sit on Pa's knee, and that made me furious. I already feared Pa, so I did not want to sit on his knee. Regardless of how much I protested the change, nobody listened to me. When the photographer insisted on making that change, he completely ruined my mood. I was determined to punish the photographer for making such an awful decision.

No matter how many funny animations he performed with his puppets, I simply refused to smile, and I continued to stare at him with a scowl on my face. I never in my life saw a photographer try harder to get all of us children to smile, but no way would I cooperate by giving him what he wanted. Why should I? He did not give me what I wanted.

LUMPY OATMEAL

I already feared Pa when I was a toddler in a high chair. My first memory of his abuse was at the breakfast table when I was two.

Ma often made oatmeal for breakfast. It was difficult to swallow because it was usually lumpy, with big chunks of oats that were clumped together.

By then, Ma already had seven children, one right after the other, so it is no wonder she might not have had the time to properly stir the oatmeal while it was cooking on the stove. With that many children, no doubt, she must have been struggling to adjust to her rapidly increasing workload.

If I had enough time to chew Ma's lumpy oatmeal before swallowing, I had no problem. When Pa was in the house, however, that never happened. He always wanted me to swallow every spoon of the oatmeal "now, right now," and he did not allow me enough time to chew it first. By attempting to swallow it before chewing, I gagged on the lumpy parts.

Whenever I coughed it back up again, Pa became unreasonably angry and tried to force me to swallow my oatmeal even faster. Pa then held my baby hands down on the high chair tray and pounded my knuckles with the heavy handle end of a table knife, while yelling at me to swallow. If I could have, I would have, because having my knuckles pounded hurt so badly. Going through Pa's torment only made matters worse, and I got so nervous that I gagged on the lumpy oatmeal even more.

To avoid going through that struggle every morning, I tried to get Ma to feed me breakfast early before Pa got done milking the cows and doing his other morning chores in the barn. Sometimes, Ma let me eat before Pa got into the house, and if I was not done yet, she allowed me to quickly hide my bowl of oatmeal in the ice box, which is where we kept food cold before we had a refrigerator.

Ever since I went through that trauma as a toddler, seeing a table knife automatically causes me to relive that experience. I can never get through a single day without seeing a table knife, so I am constantly reminded of it every day of my life.

Worst of all, throughout most of my adult life, I couldn't eat oatmeal without gagging and vomiting, even when it was properly cooked and did not have lumps. When I was a young mother, Quaker Oats came out with those packets of instant oatmeal in many different flavors, and I wanted to eat them, but I couldn't. Instead, I could only watch my sons enjoy eating their favorite flavored oatmeal.

At one point, I sought help from a professional hypnotist. After my first session, he said the trauma I suffered was so great that it would probably take at least ten sessions for the hypnosis to do me any good. I couldn't afford to pay for that many sessions, so I gave up. Later, I learned about a different kind of oatmeal called steel-cut oats. As long as it did not taste anything like Ma's oatmeal, I thought it might work, and it did. When I was sixty-five, I was able to eat oatmeal for the first time since I was a child. Steel-cut oats did not make me sick. That was a huge victory!

PA CHOKES MA

I never liked the nursery rhyme and lullaby song "Rock-a-Bye Baby" because of the lyrics: "When the bough breaks, the cradle will fall, and down will come baby, cradle and all." I did not think it was a soothing message to be singing to babies and toddlers, but that is the song I heard most often throughout my childhood years. I liked that song even less when I saw some of those lyrics come true before my eyes.

When I was two years old, I was standing in the dining room when Ma and Pa got into a horrible argument. I just wanted them to stop. Ma was standing next to my baby sister Ann, who was sitting in a high chair.

Suddenly, Pa went berserk and wrapped his big leathery hands around Ma's neck. He had the fierce look of a wild animal in his eyes, just like a boa constrictor snake about to squeeze the life out of its prey. I was terrified and didn't know what to do to make Pa stop choking Ma. In her struggle to get away, Ma purposely kicked the high chair over, sending Ann crashing to the floor. When I saw that, I remembered the words to the lullaby, "Down will come baby, cradle and all," but they got the lyrics wrong because the wind and cradle had nothing to do with it. Instead it was, "When Pa tries to kill Ma, down will come baby, high chair and all." I was worried Ann might be badly hurt, but at least Pa let go of Ma's neck to pick up my screaming baby sister. That gave Ma the chance to run out of the house, leaving me and Ann there—alone and unprotected from our monster of a father. Surprisingly, I still dared to talk.

"Where did Mama go?" I asked. "I want Mama."

"We do not care where Mama went," Pa said.

"Is Mama going to come back home?"

"No, I hope Mama never comes back home," Pa said. "We do not need your mama. She can stay gone, for all I care."

I don't know where my older brothers and sisters were when this happened. After Ann stopped crying, Pa put her down and went outside. I was so frightened because I did not know if we would ever see Ma again. I took Ann into our bedroom closet and closed the door. I told her we needed to be very quiet and hide there in the dark so Pa would not hurt us. I do not remember how long we stayed there.

Ma was gone for what seemed like several days, and I was beginning to think she would never return. Pa did the cooking, and he burned nearly everything, but we always had to eat whatever he made, anyway.

One day when Pa was gone with my big brother Tom, Ma came back with her mother and two brothers. They loaded the five of us kids into a car—all of us except for Tom. I heard Ma's brother question whether or not they should wait there to take Tom with us, too, but Ma wanted to leave right away.

Before we left, Pa suddenly showed up, and Ma then wanted to take Tom, too, but they let him choose. Tom chose to stay and help Pa on the farm. He was the firstborn, and Pa treated him better than us other kids.

We then went to Grandma Marion's house and stayed there for what seemed like a couple weeks. The food was so good, everybody was so nice, and it was so peaceful and quiet. I wanted to stay there forever. Unfortunately, Pa showed up one day, and I knew it would ruin everything. For some stupid reason, Ma agreed to go back with him to the farm.

As an adult, I asked Ma why she went back to Pa after he nearly choked her to death.

"I had no other choice," Ma said. "My mother telephoned your father and asked him to come and get us because she couldn't afford to feed so many mouths. With only an eighth-grade education, I couldn't get a good enough job to support all of you kids.

"But it was mostly the Catholic priest's fault," she added. "He told us that we would both surely go to hell if we ever got divorced."

"But you were already in hell," I said.

"At least the priest made Pa take me on a late honeymoon trip," Ma said.

Yeah, when Ma said "late," she really meant it. How many couples would take six children with them and call it a honeymoon? Well, that's exactly what Ma and Pa did. When they went on that long "honeymoon" road trip to Yellowstone National Park, Mount Rushmore, and Wall Drug, my sister Katherine was deceased, and as a two-year-old, I was next to the youngest.

One night Ma and Pa couldn't find a motel where we

could stay, so we all had to sleep in the car. Another night our parents slept in a big, new tent with another adult couple, our friends the Merks, who went on the trip with us. All of us kids were stuck sleeping in an old, dilapidated, tattered tent that leaked. The next morning, the tent smelled like a garbage dump because we all got bad cases of diarrhea. Poop was on everything and everyone—us, our clothes, the bedding, and the tent. I remember the cleanup process took nearly a full day.

Even the adults got sick from the bad water everyone drank the day before, and they were having difficulty sharing the one and only bathroom facility available.

I also remember hiking behind the adults up a dirt path going all the way up to see the heads on Mount Rushmore. They were finished on October 31, 1941. When we were there in 1949, visitors were still allowed to get close. I even saw a photo of Pa standing inside the mouth of one of the heads.

On the hike up there, Ma carried baby Ann, but as a two-year-old, I was on my own. I wanted an adult to hold my hand or carry me because the dirt path was close to the edge of what looked like a rather steep cliff. I had a hard time walking fast enough to stay with the grown-ups. I vividly remember being very afraid that I might fall hundreds of feet down the cliff. I don't know how I managed to walk all the way up there with no help.

We also visited Wall Drug. Everybody continued walking ahead of me, and again, I tried to keep up with the others. At one point, all of the adults turned a corner, disappeared, and left me behind. As I looked up, I saw a huge lifelike grizzly bear standing up on its hind feet with its big claws and paws above me. The bear's mouth was wide open, and its sharp teeth made it look like it was about to attack and eat a frightened little girl for dinner. In fact, I was so scared I was unable to yell or move.

Finally, somebody came back to look for me. Ma and Pa found me frozen in place, staring up at that fierce-looking, lifelike grizzly bear display. To me, that was one of the most frightening experiences of my life, but my parents thought it was funny. I never did understand how they could laugh about it while telling other people how terrified I was of that grizzly bear display. As a two-year-old, I felt my life was in danger, and no one was there to protect me. I never saw humor in that, so it irritated me when my parents laughed about it.

PA PUSHES MA FROM A MOVING CAR

One day when I was two years old, I was riding in the backseat of our Hudson car along with my sister Pat. Ma was in the front passenger seat, holding my baby sister Ann, when Ma and Pa got into a huge argument.

While driving down a gravel country road on the way to the grocery store, Pa reached over and slapped Ma. At this point, my sister Pat and I have different memories of what happened next. My memory saw Pa open the car door, pushing and forcing Ma and the baby from the car while it was still moving. Pat's memory saw Ma open the car door herself and leap from the moving car with the baby still in her arms.

In later years, I asked Ma if she was pushed from the car or if she voluntarily jumped from the moving vehicle. She insisted that Pa pushed her out. I doubt Pa could have reached far enough across the seat to open the door, so my sister and

I might both be partly right. Ma most likely opened the car door herself and threatened to jump out, and then Pa pushed her. Regardless, we both saw Ma rolling down into a ditch that was filled with barbed wire fencing with our baby sister still in her arms. Pat and I both begged Pa to turn around and go back to see if Ma and the baby were hurt. Instead, without even looking back, Pa coldly and boldly continued driving into town to do the shopping. I still remember my panic like it was yesterday. My two-year-old memory draws a blank, however, as to whether either of them was injured, or how they got back home.

APPLES AND PEARS

I vividly remember the day I learned the difference between apples and pears.

We had several apple trees and a few pear trees on our farm in Braham, Minnesota. When I was three years old, I looked out my open bedroom window and saw my big brother Tom eating an apple. I called out to him and asked him to get me an apple, too.

"I want that really good-tasting kind of apple," I said. A few minutes later, he brought me a big red apple.

"No, this is the wrong kind," I said.

"Well, that's the best-tasting apple we have," Tom said.

"But the kind of apple I want is green."

Tom looked surprised. "Green?" he asked. "Are you sure? Those green apples don't taste very good. They are not sweet. They're bitter."

But I insisted I wanted the green kind, so he went back to the apple orchard and soon returned with a green apple.

When Tom handed me the green apple, I said, "No, no, no! This is still the wrong kind."

"Well, those are the only kind of green apples we have," Tom said. "We don't have any other kind of apples!"

"Oh yes, we do," I said. "I want the kind with the bump on one end."

Tom laughed. "Oh, the ones with the bump on the end are pears, not apples, silly!"

"Then bring me a pear," I said.

That was the day I learned the difference between apples and pears.

THE GRANARY

By the time I was four years old, I already knew what I would have to do—get tough or die. In fact, I remember the very moment I came to that conclusion.

One day, when all of my older brothers and sisters were in school, Pa came to the house and asked Ma to put my snowsuit on me because he needed my help outside. Ma never asked him what he was going to have me do. She just bundled me up and handed me over. Perhaps that was a sign of the times when women were taught to obey their husbands, no questions asked.

Pa took me to the granary on our farm. A wide conveyor belt was hooked up from the tractor pulley outside to the pulley on the hammer mill inside the granary. The upper part of the granary had a built-in grain bin. Directly above the hammer mill was a little sliding door in the floor of the grain bin, big enough when open to easily slip a little girl like me through the hole.

When the grain bin was full of oats, Pa opened the sliding

door, and the oats would fall into the mouth of the hammer mill. At the same time, Pa shoveled scoops of what looked like flour to be ground up along with the oats. That day the grain bin was no longer full. Oats were still left in the grain bin, but they now formed a big "V," and oats no longer came out on their own when the sliding door was open.

After Pa lifted me up and put me through the hole in the floor of the grain bin, I looked down and saw many sharp, thin, knife-like blades at the open mouth of the hammer mill located directly underneath the hole. The hammer mill was usually referred to as the feeder because it was used to grind feed, which was part of the process used to make pig slop to fatten up the hogs for market. Pa said my job would be to push oats through the hole as quickly as I could as soon as he started the machine.

When I attempted to crawl higher up on the oats to get away from the open hole, I discovered my snowsuit was rather slippery, so I looked around for a rope or something to hold onto. As I started sliding, I called down to Pa to ask him what I could hold onto.

"You don't need anything to hold onto," he hollered. "Just keep pushing the oats down as fast as you can as soon as I start it up."

Even though I was young, I realized that if I slid through that hole, I would be chopped into little pieces before Pa could possibly have enough reaction time to shut down the machine. When Pa started it, I saw those knife-like blades chopping away at such a high speed they looked like a blur. Later models of the hammer mill had sharp little teeth instead of blades.

"Okay, push the oats down," Pa hollered.

Pa continually yelled at me to push more oats through the

hole faster and faster.

As soon as I started pushing some of the oats down into the moving blades of the hammer mill, I slid farther down. I was terrified.

"You need to push the oats down faster," Pa yelled.

I started pushing the oats as quickly as I could. I noticed there was a blank spot on the bin floor on each side of the hole. Suddenly, I felt myself sliding directly toward the hole. At the last moment, I did the splits, landing one foot on each side of the hole, just barely stopping myself from falling into the mouth of the hammer mill along with the oats.

At that moment, while staring into those moving blades a few feet from my face, I knew I had to do something to protect and save myself because nobody else would. To stay safe, I would have to get tough or die. That meant I would have to ignore Pa no matter how much he hollered at me to work faster. I would work only as fast as I knew I could without falling through the hole.

After what seemed like an eternity, Pa finally had enough ground feed, so he shut down the hammer mill and lifted me down from the oats bin. Before taking me back into the house, he stood in the doorway of the granary watching the first snowfall of the year as he talked about the weather and how it would affect his crops.

I remember thinking that just a few minutes before I narrowly escaped falling into the sharp blades of the hammer mill, and Pa could have lost his precious little girl to a tragic accident, but all he talked about was the weather. That did not make sense to me. I knew then that he must have cared more about his crops and making money than he cared about me.

COAL FURNACE FIRE

Anyone who has spent a winter in Minnesota knows the meaning of the word *cold*, especially if they're in the state during a 60-degree-below-zero windchill.

The winter when I was four years old, we were having one of those awful cold winter days, and not much heat was coming out of our registers, so our Braham farmhouse got rather chilly. By that time, I was the fifth eldest out of seven children. We had a coal furnace in our basement and a big pile of coal on the basement floor. Most of the time, Pa or my oldest brother, Tom, would shovel the coal into the furnace. It was no easy task to scoop up big, heavy shovels of coal and sling them into the furnace, but Tom, a nine-year-old, could do it. He was the oldest and also much bigger, more muscular, and stronger than my other brother, Bernie, eight, who was smaller for his age.

Both Pa and Tom had gone somewhere that cold winter day, so Ma asked Bernie if he thought he was big and strong enough to shovel a few scoops of coal into the furnace. Bernie had never done that job before, but he appeared to be proud and happy that he was being trusted to do his big brother's job.

Ma had never explained to Bernie that there was a limit to how much coal he should shovel into the furnace. Most likely, she underestimated his ability to do the job. Bernie, on the other hand, saw this as an opportunity to prove himself. He wanted to prove to Ma that he could shovel coal just as well as, if not better than, his brother. So Bernie added a couple shovels full of coal into the furnace, and then he went far beyond that and added *several* more shovels of coal.

When Bernie finished, he told me what a good job he had done, and how everyone would be very surprised. A short time later, everyone was surprised all right, but not in a good way.

Soon we had a major emergency. The next thing I remember is standing at the top of the stairs, looking down into our basement, seeing the heat ducts broken in half with huge flames of fire shooting out. I saw Pa down there in a panic, trying to gain control of the situation.

He got home just in time to fix it and prevent a house fire, but for several intense minutes, it was pure pandemonium.

That night at the supper table, Pa was furious. He lectured Bernie over and over about how wrong it was for him to shovel that much coal into the furnace. He said the furnace burned so hot that it melted the metal at the seams that held the heat ducts together, causing them to break.

I felt so sorry for Bernie because he worked so hard only to see his plan backfire. He was trying to prove to Ma and Pa that he was just as valuable and deserving of love as Tom.

GUN TRAUMA

When I was five years old, a man grabbed me, pinned me down on a sofa, held a gun to my head, and said he was going to kill me. My eyes desperately searched the room for someone … anyone … to stop him. Other siblings in the room stood frozen in place, fearing my tormentor might turn the rifle on them.

Then I caught a glimpse of Ma sitting in a chair nearby. As I looked in her direction with pleading eyes to save me, I realized she was the one who put him up to it. I closed my eyes tightly and waited for the fatal shot. I heard the sound of the trigger, but the final blast never came. All that followed was laughter—the insane laughter of a man who was delighted at the terror in my face. That man was my father.

"You will never get a chance to kill your mother because I am going to kill you first," Pa yelled as he looked at me with the eyes of a madman. I knew that Ma told Pa only part of what happened earlier that day—only the part she wanted him to hear, not the whole story, but I knew I would never get a chance to tell him my part. Pa never gave any of his children the chance to explain. We had no voice, and we had no rights. We were just numbers. I was number six out of ten at the time.

Pa then proceeded to whack me hard across my pale baby face with his big, leathery hands, giving me a bloody nose, dripping blood onto my favorite white sailor dress.

"Now you will go outside to the garden and pull every weed in the strawberry patch," Pa ordered. "You will not be allowed to come back to the house until you are done, even if it takes you all night."

Considering the size of our 100-foot-long garden and huge strawberry patch, I thought it might take that long, too, even if I were the fastest five-year-old weed-puller in the country.

I went out to the garden feeling lucky to be alive, but at the same time thinking I might be better off dead. Immediately, I felt the unbearable Minnesota summer sun beating down. I hated the unbearably hot summers and the extremely cold winters. With blood and tears streaming down my cheeks, I thought how nice it would be to have some gloves to protect my dainty little hands from those awful stickers mixed in with the weeds.

Soon after, my eight-year-old sister Pat came outside with a piece of cotton to plug my nostril and stop my nosebleed.

Then she gave me a drink of cold water. I felt so grateful for my big sister that day.

Pat saw what really happened when she walked into the room earlier that day. She knew what made me say those awful words, and she knew I did not mean them. They were words said in a moment of desperation—the same words I often heard other siblings say when they got into squabbles—words I thought might shock Ma into stopping what she was doing.

The day had started out just fine. I saw some of my siblings doing headstands on the sofa, kicking their feet up against the wall. It looked like fun, so I did it, too. Suddenly, I felt a whack on my bare bottom.

"Shame on you, young lady, for doing headstands with no bloomer pants on," Ma said. "Why aren't you wearing any panties?"

"I could not find any, Mama," I said.

"Well, I just washed a pair, and they are in the laundry basket in that bedroom," she said, while pointing her finger. "Get in there right now and put some bloomers on."

I quickly ran into the bedroom and started digging through the huge laundry basket full of clothes. After digging through the clothes, I still could not find any little girl's underwear, so I went to the kitchen to try to get Mama to help. That was a big mistake. That is when my "fine day" first started turning into one of the worst days of my life.

In those days, farm families usually had four meals a day—breakfast, dinner, lunch, and supper. The noon meal was dinner. Ma was busy making dinner, nearly tripping over one of my younger siblings crawling around on the kitchen floor.

"You kids go play somewhere else before I end up spilling

hot grease on you," Ma said. She then turned to me and asked, "Now what do you want? Did you put your bloomers on yet?"

"No, Mama, I looked and looked and still cannot find them," I said.

"Oh, and I suppose you expect me to help you find them when I am busy making dinner," she said. That's when Ma really lost it. Slamming a pan of mashed potatoes down on the stove, she grabbed me by the hand and stormed off into the bedroom. Digging through the laundry basket, she soon found my panties and threw them at me.

"Here they are. I told you they were there, and you got me away from my work for nothing," she screamed as she pushed me to the floor. Before I could even put the panties on, Ma started jumping up and down directly above me like a crazy woman. I rolled back and forth on the floor in an effort to avoid being stomped to death by her feet. As I rolled around, I pleaded with her to stop.

"I'm sorry, I'm sorry, I couldn't find them," I said. "Please stop, please stop, Mama, please stop!"

Instead, Ma appeared to have a complete mental breakdown, jumping up and down even closer to my little body, just narrowly missing me several times. I feared I would be stomped to death by a full-grown adult—my own mother, who had momentarily gone mad.

Finally, in desperation, I yelled, "Stop, stop it, or I'll kill you!" As soon as those words came out of my mouth, I was just as shocked as Ma was, but at least it made her stop.

Before leaving the room, she turned to me and said, "Just you wait until I tell your father what you said, young lady. You'll be sorry you ever said that. I will make you so sorry."

I got up to put my panties on and saw my big sister Pat

standing in the doorway of the bedroom. She apparently interrupted the situation. Pat gave me a hug, dried my tears, washed my face, and combed my hair.

"Look, I found your favorite sailor dress," she said. "Let's put this one on you. I will dress you up pretty, and then we can go upstairs to play dolls. You can pretend you are my real-live doll." Pat took me by the hand, and we went upstairs. She made me feel like I was valued, loved, and safe again; she helped me to put my horrifying experience with Ma behind me. A short time later, however, I heard Pa and my big brothers come into the house, and we were all called to the table for dinner. When I saw Ma sit next to Pa at the far end of our long table, I remembered her threat and got very frightened, so I tried to eat quickly so I could go back upstairs to hide. Before I got a chance to leave, Pa turned to my oldest brother Tom.

"Go out to the shed and bring me the rifle," Pa said. "I am going to use it to kill your sister Barbara to teach her and the rest of you a lesson that you cannot talk to your mother like she did."

"No, Pa, no … I don't want to get the gun," Tom pleaded.

"You do as I say, right now!" Pa said. "You get that rifle, or I will get it myself and use it on you, too!"

It surprised me to hear Pa threaten Tom, his firstborn—the son he always favored and treated so much better than the rest of us. Tom hesitated, but he went outside to get the gun. I'll never forget the scared look on Tom's face when he handed the rifle over to Pa. Tom only did what he had to do. He had no choice, so I did not blame him.

Later, I learned that Tom checked the gun to make sure it had no shells in the chamber before he brought it into the house and handed it over to Pa. That is why it did not fire.

Was Pa aware the gun was not loaded? That is something I'll never know, but I feel certain that he was fully prepared to kill me that day, and it was only by an act of God that my life was spared.

As the hours passed and I toiled away in the garden, it was beginning to get dark, and the weeds were getting more difficult to see. I wondered if I would be better off if I ran away as far as I could go and never came back. I thought about my neighbor friend Genevieve and how lucky she was because her daddy was a really kind man who spoke in a calm voice. He smiled a lot, too, and I often saw him hug and kiss his wife and children. They were not afraid of him. He was the kind of Pa I wanted, too.

About 10 p.m. Tom came outside to tell me I was supposed to come back in the house because it was getting too dark for me to see the weeds, and I might accidentally pull up some of the strawberry vines. I would, however, have to get up early the next morning to finish the job.

By that time, my fingers were aching, and I was hungry from missing supper, but I almost thought it would be better to stay out in the garden all night than to go back into the house near Pa and a mother who failed to protect me. Isn't that what Ma was for—to protect her children?

Me (left) at age four and Ann, three, were wearing our new dresses and Easter bonnets. My bonnet was navy blue, and my dress was light blue. Anne's bonnet was white, and her dress was pink. We were the same ages here that we were when we ran away from home.

RUNAWAY
GIRLS

WHEN I WAS FOUR YEARS OLD, we often visited the Anderson family, who had a farm about four miles from ours.

I loved visiting the Andersons because they always gave me special treats like cookies and roasted marshmallows. Even better, their daughter Alice, about ten years old, had a bedroom that was the nearest thing to a toy store I had ever seen.

Alice was pretty, with golden blonde hair cascading down in ringlet curls, much like young Shirley Temple's hairstyle, and she was always dressed like a fairy princess in a storybook.

Her older sister Donna, who was in high school, was plain looking. She was tall and slender with short dark hair and horn-rimmed glasses.

Mr. Anderson appeared to be about six feet three inches tall and had a husky build. He was always gentle and kind toward his wife and children.

Whenever I visited at the Andersons' house, I was not allowed to touch any of Alice's porcelain dolls, but she always let me play with her long-handled blue purse with a doll face on the front of it and her toy chicken that laid eggs when I pushed down on its feet.

One day, I heard Pa say that he was going to stop at the Andersons' farm on his way back from town, so I wanted to go, too. As he was leaving, I begged Pa to let me go, too, but he refused to take me.

"No, you cannot go; you have to stay home," Pa said as he pushed me back and drove away. Lying on the ground, I started to cry—until I remembered what Mrs. Anderson told me a few weeks earlier:

"Some day when you are big enough, your mother might let you walk to our house all by yourself to visit us."

At that moment, I knew I was already big enough, but I did not think Ma would agree.

Ma had already bundled me and my three-year-old sister Ann up in our coats and put us outside to play, so we would not be underfoot while she cleaned the house. Ann and I usually played on a swing hanging from a tree branch near the front of the house.

As soon as I decided to walk to the Andersons' farm, I knew I would have to take Ann with me because she could get hurt if I left her there all alone. So I told her about my plan.

"I don't want to go because we might get lost," Ann said.

"No, we won't get lost because I know the way really good," I said. "All we have to do is walk to the end of this long driveway, then turn this way." I gestured to the left. "Then go up and down three big hills on the long gravel road. At the end of that road, we will come to a black smooth road, and then we will turn this way again. After we go a little farther on the smooth road, we will see another dirt road on the other side, and then if we walk down that dirt road, we will see the Andersons' house. See, I know the way really good, so we won't get lost!"

"But Mommy will see us because sometimes she looks out the window at us," Ann said.

"Well, I have a plan on how we can sneak away without her seeing us," I said. "Let's just wait until the next time she looks out the window at us. Then when she's done looking, we will have enough time to walk really fast to the driveway. By the time Mommy looks out the window again, we will already be walking in the ditch, and she won't see us because the grass is really tall, and we are so little."

I had to do an awful lot of talking to convince Ann I would not get us lost and that walking to the Andersons' farm was a good idea. Even after we started walking, Ann kept trying to persuade me to turn around and go back home.

"I'm scared of that big man," she said.

"Oh, you don't have to be afraid of him. He just looks scary, but he's a really nice big man. He will even give us marshmallows, and they taste really good."

"But what if their big dogs knock us down and try to bite us?" she asked.

I had forgotten about the dogs at the Andersons' house until Ann reminded me about them.

"Don't worry," I said. "If those mean dogs try to knock us down and bite us, the Andersons will run out of their house and save us."

I never thought about what could happen if the Andersons were not at home to rescue us, or I would have been too afraid to continue.

I also had no idea how dangerous it was for two little girls to be walking all alone down a country road. Luckily, we saw only a few cars, and I always told Ann we had to hide until the cars passed and were out of sight. Once we hid behind some bales of hay near the side of the road, and another time we hid by lying down in the tall grass. I didn't want to take any chances of anybody seeing us. I was not aware of the danger of two little girls walking down the road alone. I was just afraid someone might stop to take us back home again, ruining my plans to have fun.

When we arrived at the Anderson farm, those two big dogs barked loudly and ran straight for us. I was so relieved when the Andersons came outside in time to call them off and save us.

"How did you get here?" Mrs. Anderson asked.

"Oh, we just walked," I said.

"Did your parents drop you off at the driveway?" Mrs. Anderson asked.

"No," I said. "We just walked. We walked all the way from our house to your house. Mommy said I'm big enough to come and visit you all by myself, and she let me bring my little sister Ann with me."

I immediately got the impression they did not believe me. It was a really big lie for a four-year-old.

"We didn't know you were coming," Mrs. Anderson said. "What time did your mother say you would have to go home?"

I did not like that question, because I didn't know how to tell time yet, and I was afraid I might give them the wrong number on the clock. I wanted to stay and play for a long time, and I did not want to take any chances of having to go home too soon.

"What time did your mother say you have to go home?" Mrs. Anderson asked again.

I thought that was a trick question to trap me into giving them a wrong answer.

"I'm not going to tell," I said. "I'm just not going to tell."

Then Mrs. Anderson got Mr. Anderson to ask me the same question, and he tried to bribe me to answer by giving me a roasted marshmallow.

"I'm not going to tell … I'm just not going to tell." I thought that answer was working, so I was sticking with it.

After trying to get an answer from me for several minutes, the Andersons finally looked at each other with a defeated smile and released me to go play.

While we were playing, our Pa stopped by the Andersons' farm on his way back from town, like he said he would.

"Your father is here," Alice said. "If you don't believe me, just come over here and look out the window."

At first, I didn't want to look out the window for fear Pa might see me. But I thought Alice might just be teasing me, so I took a quick peek. Sure enough, Pa's truck was outside. I quickly stepped back from the window because I thought my big brother Tom, who was sitting in the truck, could have seen me peeking, and I was not ready to go back home.

In fact, I never wanted to go back home. I told Mr. Anderson that I wanted him to be my new daddy so I could stay there all the time.

"Oh, wouldn't you miss your own daddy?" he asked.

"No," I said. "He is mean to me, so I want you to be my new daddy."

"Well, don't you think your parents would miss you?"

"No, because they already have a lot of other children," I said.

"Wouldn't you even miss your mother?" he asked.

"Yes, I would miss her a little, but you could take me to visit her sometimes," I said.

I was really worried when Pa was at the Andersons' farm that he might come into the house and see me and Ann there.

Later I learned that Tom did see me peeking out the window, but our parents did not believe him. They said it would be impossible for two little girls to walk that far. My parents often underestimated what I could do.

"You are not supposed to be over here, are you?" Alice asked. "Your mother doesn't know that you are here, does she?"

I refused to answer, and I was already looking for a place to hide in case Pa came into the house. Thankfully, he never did. I was glad when he drove away.

I just wanted Alice to keep her big mouth shut before anyone else heard her speaking the truth. Surprisingly, nobody told Pa that we were there. The Andersons already had a telephone, but my parents did not, so as soon as Pa left, I knew I was safe to stay and play for the rest of the day.

After dark, the Andersons were not about to send us two little girls back home by ourselves, so they asked their daughter Donna to drive us home in their Model-T Ford.

All the way home, I worried about what would happen when we got there. I knew I would be in trouble for sneaking away without permission.

When we arrived, I saw Pa standing near the barn with a milk pail in his hand. I heard him yelling to my eight-year-old brother Bernie.

"Did you find those girls yet?"

"No," Bernie said.

"Then get right back into those woods and keep looking for them," Pa said.

As I was getting out of the car, I saw the terrified look on Bernie's face. I was so glad he would not have to go back into those dark woods.

When Ma saw us, she grabbed Ann and showered her with hugs and kisses.

"Where on Earth did you find these girls?" she asked Donna.

Donna told her how I said I had permission to visit, and the only welcome home I got was a good scolding. Then I got sent to bed with no supper. Ann, on the other hand, got something to eat. It was obvious to me my parents cared a lot more for her than they did for me.

So I went to sleep, hungry, but with a great big smile on my face. After all, I found my way to the Andersons' house all by myself, and I outsmarted all of the grown-ups. I did not allow them to trick me into saying the wrong time, and I had a really fun day. I felt really proud of myself, even if nobody else did.

Yet, I never ran away from home again—not because of the scolding, or because I went without supper. I simply did not want Bernie to go into those dark woods to look for us again. As a little girl, I already knew it was far too scary and might be dangerous for such a young boy to wander around in the woods alone. Why didn't Ma and Pa know that?

Aerial view of the family farm taken by the Pope County Tribune in 1954, before the barn was doubled in size and a two-car garage was built next to the house. Most of the buildings were burned in a fire in September 1967.

Some of us, oldest to youngest, sitting in the corn elevator. I'm the fifth from the top.

SLAVE LABOR

ONE DAY, Pa lined about eight of us kids up and asked, "Do you think I had you kids to help me spend my money? No, I had you to help me make money."

I already suspected that, but it surprised me when Pa came right out and said it. He had us for his own financial gain, and he didn't care if we knew it. Lots of farmers had large families for that purpose—to do the farmwork so they wouldn't have to hire help. However, most farmers loved their families, too.

This is what my brother Buzz had to say about it:

We hated all the work. Feeding cattle and hogs, cleaning barns, doing field work, and staying up all night helping sows deliver piglets. We had a 2,000-pound bull. The Old Man used to let him

*out while we cleaned the barn so he could breed
the cows that were in heat. He was mean, so we
boys had to carry a 2 x 4 when we went to the
granary so we could whack him in the nose when
he came after us. The Old Man told us we had to
spread the straw out nice and even in the bull's 12
x 12-foot pen when he was in there instead of just
throwing it over the fence. You had to be quick.*

Buzz said all of those chores usually amounted to fifty-four hours a week while they were still in school.

My brothers usually had more hard work to do outside, but we all had chores to do. Pa always left a list of chores for Ma to give us, like orders from headquarters, as soon as we got home from school and changed into our work clothes.

I seldom got a chance to start doing my school assignments until about 10 p.m., and I never remember going to bed before midnight. I often fell asleep on my books, and I usually had a hard time staying awake in school.

Because the Catholic religion required it, Sundays were usually a day of rest. They were our only chance to have a few free hours to try to enjoy life. This is what Buzz wrote about it:

*Sometimes we ran the five miles round-trip to the
nearest lake to fish and swim. Once in a while
we went over to our nearest neighbor's place and
hung out with Stevie T. That was a treat. Stevie
was an only child. His mother was a teacher, and
his dad farmed. They loved and nurtured their
son. He was pudgy and of average intelligence,
but he had their respect. There were never harsh*

words or beatings. He had good food and didn't
have to wear rummage sale rags. His parents were
my role models.

I believe most of us sought out and found role models out-side of our home so we could have better examples of how life was supposed to be lived.

FIRST JOBS

As soon as my siblings and I could walk, we had jobs to do every day.

When I was four years old, Ma told me it would be my job every morning to make up all the beds in the house while all my older brothers and sisters were in school. Because she was a full-grown adult, all she had to do was stand on the side of the bed, flap the sheets and blankets up and down a few times, and let them float down into place.

I did not understand why she didn't make the beds her-self, since it took her only a few minutes, but it took me all morning. As a little girl, I had to crawl all over the top of the beds while pulling the corners of the sheets and blankets to each end of the bed, and then I had to crawl around on top of the beds to pull all the wrinkles out. It was so frustrating because every time I pulled the wrinkles out of one side, the other side got more wrinkles. But that was my job, and I was not allowed to play until my job was done. Oftentimes, Ma gave me other jobs, too.

For example, one day Ma moved an ice box, which is what people used to keep food cold before refrigerators became common household appliances. Behind the ice box, the green plastic squares on the wall were filthy dirty, nearly black from smoke and soot. Ma gave me a small bucket of water, a washcloth, Dutch Cleanser, and a stool to stand on to reach the high parts. She showed me that by putting some cleanser onto a wet washcloth, I could wipe the tiles clean and make them look like new again. It was my job to clean that entire section of wall. It was a tedious job for a little girl, but when I finished, I remember feeling a strong sense of accomplishment and pride in my work. Even Ma was amazed at how well I had done.

DRIVING TRACTOR

When my older brothers and sisters were all in school, I was the oldest preschooler still at home. That meant as a four-year-old, I had to help Pa with jobs he needed done on the farm. The first time Pa sat me on top of a wobbly metal tractor seat, I was afraid I might fall off and get run over by one of the two big tractor wheels on each side.

Pa told me it was my job to steer, making sure the two front tires of the tractor stayed between the rows of corn, while he loaded corn stalks onto the wagon. If I ran over any corn, Pa would stop, pull me off the tractor, and give me a spanking. I was terrified.

Many times, my siblings and I were put on a full-size Oliver tractor and ordered to steer it before we were even old enough, heavy enough, or tall enough to put the clutch down to stop it.

When I was ten years old, Pa put me on a tractor and ordered me to drive it down a dirt road out to a field about two miles away. He told me not to worry about stopping it because he would follow me in his truck in a few minutes, pass me on his way out, and jump onto the tractor when I got there. After he sent me on my way, Pa got distracted fixing some machinery and forgot all about me. When I arrived, I didn't know what to do. I wasn't heavy enough to push the clutch down, and I did not know how to stop the tractor. I thought about turning around and driving the tractor back to the farmhouse again, but I thought Pa would be upset, so I did the next best thing. I drove the tractor around in circles waiting for Pa to arrive, but he never did.

After several hours, the tractor ran out of diesel fuel and finally stopped. There I was—stuck two miles out in the field in the pitch dark. I climbed down from the tractor and ran back down the single-lane dirt road. About halfway back, I heard a hooting noise that startled me. It was a huge white owl sitting on a fence post a few feet away, looking straight at me with its huge eyes. I'll never forget that image. Never before, or since, had I ever gotten that close to an owl.

CORN SILO

Every fall Pa filled our forty-foot concrete silo with chopped corn, called silage, used to feed cattle during the winter months. My brothers climbed up, using the window door handles as a ladder, to throw silage down the chute to feed the cows. As the silage supply got lower, more window doors were taken down, so there were fewer doors to climb.

When I was six years old, Pa put me on his back and climbed about three-fourths of the way up because that's how full our silo was at the time. When we reached the top open window, Pa put me inside, where I saw a string of wide pipes dangling down from the center hole of the steel dome. A thick rope was attached to the pipes. Pa told me he was going to unload two wagons of corn stalks, and my job was to continuously pull that rope around in circles to spread the silage around. Otherwise, it would get backed up and plug the pipes. If I let that happen, I would get a whipping.

Outside the silo, a tight conveyor belt ran from the tractor to what we called the silo-filler (ensilage cutter). It had pipes attached to one end that ran straight up to the top of the silo, and those pipes were attached to more pipes that hung down inside the silo. I never figured out what forced the silage to go straight up forty feet through those outside pipes, but I always thought it was really amazing.

I knew it was going to be a strenuous job because it wasn't easy for a young girl like me to pull those heavy pipes around, especially for long periods of time. My skinny, little arms were soon aching so badly they felt like they would fall off. Yet I did not dare to give myself a rest or stop because I was so afraid of getting spanked. At the very least, I was hoping I would get a short break to rest when Pa got done emptying the first wagon load of corn stalks before he started on the second one. No such luck. Pa was a nonstop worker, and more and more silage just continued to come out like gang-busters.

Finally, I knew I could not continue to pull those pipes around without giving my arms a rest. So every once in a while, I got on all fours and balanced the end pipe on my little buttocks, making the silage go in another direction.

By the time Pa finally got done, my arms were so tired and ached so badly that I could hardly hold my arms around his neck when he came up to take me back down. Yet I knew I did not want to be stuck up there for long because I heard Pa talk about dangerous gases, like nitrogen dioxide, that are formed by the natural fermentation of chopped corn.

I later learned that these gases usually reach a peak about

three days later, and they rapidly decrease after that, as long as the silo is well ventilated. Still, these colorless and odorless gases present a real danger. I know many people have died in corn silos when they became entrapped with no warning.

CHICKEN COOP

For several years, one of my regular jobs was to feed fifty chickens and gather the chicken eggs.

During winter months, the most difficult part was finding and digging up some gravel from our frozen gravel pit. The chickens needed some grit in their diet to form the egg shells. If they did not get enough grit, the egg shells would start looking more like thin skinlike membranes instead of hard outer shells.

During summer months, the greatest challenge was finding the eggs and getting them into our refrigerator before they spoiled. That was not easy when our chickens roamed free and could lay eggs anywhere on the farm, in any building. I often found chicken egg nests in the haymow of our barn, but I found egg nests in other strange places, too.

One summer I was not finding very many eggs, so I thought our chickens simply had stopped laying them. Wrong! When my brothers were feeding hay to the cattle, they uncovered a couple hundred chicken eggs that I had never found. By that time, of course, the eggs were no longer any good to eat.

I don't remember whose idea it was, but we decided to divide the spoiled eggs up, form two teams, and have an egg fight. It sounded like fun, so we set up two forts out of bales of straw about fifteen feet across from each other. That gave us something to duck behind. Unfortunately, one team had a small grain shed as a backdrop, and it happened to be located a short distance in front of the barn.

The next morning, as soon as Pa stepped out of the back door to go milk cows, his nose was immediately put to the test. With just one whiff, he said he nearly passed out. Right there in front of him the entire side of the shed was covered with splattered, dripping, rotten eggs. I don't remember any of us getting whipped for that incident, but all of us culprits were ordered to immediately wash the entire side of that building to get rid of the smell. We did our best, but the smell lingered for a long time, so we knew if we ever had another egg fight, we would have to pick a better spot the next time. Regardless, that wasn't the worst job I had when it came to the chickens.

When I was eleven years old and Ann was ten years old, Pa gave us orders that every day after school we were to chop the heads off of two chickens with an ax, pick all the feathers off, and hand the chickens over to Ma. She would then clean the gizzards out and put the plucked chickens in the freezer. That's what happened to chickens when they stopped laying eggs—they became chicken dinner. However, neither one of us young girls had any idea how to go about chopping the head off of a chicken, so we took our first chicken to one of our brothers for help. I don't remember which brother it was, but I remember what he said and did.

"Oh, you don't need the ax," he said. "All you have to do is wring the chicken's head off like this." Then he held the chicken by the head and swung it around several times until its head fell off, and the chicken's body dropped to the ground. I was shocked when the chicken started running around in circles with no head. My brother followed it while holding out its head saying, "Are you looking for this? Are you looking for this?"

We young girls were both so grossed out we decided to chop the chickens' heads off with the ax because it would be a less painful death. After we found a 2 x 4, we took turns doing the dirty work—one would hold the chicken down with its head and neck over the board, while the other one would use the ax to chop its head off.

Most of the chickens put up a big fight by flapping their wings or scratching us with their foot claws. One day, just as we were about to execute another chicken, it surprised us. The chicken did not put up a fight whatsoever. Instead, it voluntarily stretched its neck over the board, and we didn't even have to hold it down. We couldn't believe it. What we had was a chicken that wanted to die, and we felt so sorry for it that we put that chicken back and got another one. Whenever we caught the suicidal chicken, it always did the same thing, and we always put it back. That chicken outlived all the rest, and it was so nice it was the most difficult one to kill.

Another job I had was to spread fresh straw on the floor of the chicken coop every day. Eventually, the chicken manure had built up so much, layer upon layer, that no one could stand up inside the chicken coop anymore. From the floor to roof, we had crawling room only, so we had to crawl in to gather the eggs. Thankfully, the egg nests were up high enough that they were not yet buried in layers of chicken manure.

That's when Pa assigned me one of the worst chicken jobs I ever had to do: dig down through about three feet of chicken manure to find the floor again. Every day I had to take a pitchfork, dig down, and haul the chicken manure out one bucket at a time. That, my friends, was another huge, smelly job I will never forget.

ROCK PICKING

When I was about nine years old, Pa bought another eighty acres—a piece of land located a few miles from the rest of our farm. We referred to it as "the Eighty," but it was so full of rocks that we should have called it "Rocky Acres." I strongly suspect the reason Pa got such a good deal on the price of that land was because of the rocks.

For several weeks, at the top of Pa's list of after-school chores was for us to take a tractor and trailer to "the Eighty" to go rock picking. We were to pick up any rock the size of our fist or larger, load them onto a wagon until it was full, and unload them into a ditch along one edge of the property.

As we drove the tractor and trailer from one rocky spot to the next, some of us would pick rocks on one side of the open wagon, and some would pick rocks on the other side. We were such hard and fast workers that the rocks often bounced off the wagon to the other side, and yet I don't remember anyone ever getting hit in the head with those flying rocks. What a miracle!

When we removed the rocks from the field, Pa did not have to worry about damaging the blades on his plow. After Pa finished plowing, however, he turned up even more rocks for us to pick. Then we had to return to "the Eighty" to pick rocks all over again so that Pa wouldn't break the tines on his field rake.

Over the years, we picked up tons of rocks. Pa managed to turn "the Eighty" rocky acres into fertile soil that produced bumper crops.

Later, Pa built a pig house, machine shed, and two-car garage. Then we had to use those rocks from "the Eighty" for Pa to put into his foundations. By adding rocks to the foundations of his buildings, Pa did not have to use nearly as much cement. First, he dug a trench about two feet below ground and used plywood and pieces of 2 x 4s to outline the foundation about one foot above the ground. Then Pa bought several bags of cement and rented a cement mixer. He did not have to buy bags of gravel because he had his own gravel pit. To build the foundation of the buildings, Pa used bags of cement, gravel, and water. As he shoveled wet concrete into the foundation, we kids had to help by placing a rock into each new shovelful of the cement mixture. Sometimes sprinkles of splattered cement landed on my head, and it wasn't easy to get it off of my scalp and out of my hair.

OATS HARVEST

Every summer, one of the most difficult jobs my brothers and sisters and I had to do was help Pa harvest oats.

I believe Pa was one of the last farmers in the state of Minnesota to use an old-fashioned grain binder to cut the oats and a threshing machine to separate the oats from the straw. Pa would sit on the big metal seat of the grain binder next to a group of levers while it was pulled by a tractor. When the fork had about five bundles of oats on it, Pa would pull a lever to lower the fork and drop a group of oats bundles onto the ground.

While one of us children had to drive the tractor that pulled the grain binder around the field, the rest of us had to walk around the field, pick up the bundles of oats, and build them into shocks. We did that by jamming one bundle into the oats stubble and then leaning at least four other bundles all around it. When we finished making a shock, it looked like several groups of little, yellow oats tepees all over the field.

The goal was to stand those groups of bundles up well enough that they would not fall over during the first heavy rainfall. If any of the oats bundles fell over, we would have to go back out to the oats field to stand them back up again, which was more difficult when they were wet. The bundles had to dry out so they would not clog up the threshing machine.

It was backbreaking work to spend ten hours on hot summer days shocking bundles of oats weighing up to fifty pounds each. My sisters and I also got cuts on our ankles from walking through the oats stubble. Most of them were surface cuts, but it was very painful whenever they broke the skin. I don't think my brothers got as many cuts on their ankles because their legs were usually more protected by long work pants.

As difficult as it was to shock oats, the job I feared most was driving the tractor for Pa that pulled the grain binder. I was not mechanically gifted, and I knew I would get spanked at nearly every corner. It was not too difficult when I was driving in a straight row, but the corners were tricky. I never did figure out how to steer the tractor around the corners in such a way that the grain binder would pick up every strand of oats.

The only one who could do that job flawlessly was my brother Mark. He had it down to a science exactly when and how much he had to turn the steering wheel to the left, to the right, to the left, and back to the right again. Every time he came to a corner, I watched and wondered if that might be the first time he would get a whipping for missing a strand of oats, but Mark never failed—not once. In fact, he was so good at driving the tractor that some of us offered to pay him to take our turn. It did not surprise me when Mark later became a Black Hawk helicopter pilot, because he had always been mechanically gifted.

Once all of the oats fields were cut and shocked, it was threshing time. That was no easy task, either. Pa parked his big truck next to the threshing machine in the oats field. The oats would come out of a spout hanging over the bed of Pa's truck, and the straw would blow out of a thick funnel onto the ground, forming a big straw pile. I always thought the threshing machine somewhat resembled the shape of a big metal brontosaurus.

That's when the toddlers in the family, the three- and four-year-olds, had jobs, too. They were the ones who had to crawl around and spread the oats in the back of the truck bed to make sure they didn't back up in the spout and get clogged. That was a tough job for such young children because the oats didn't stop coming until the truck bed was full.

The entire operation usually involved three work crews and three tractors and wagons. Pa was a crew of one. He stayed by the threshing machine unloading bundles of oats into the thresher as it separated the oats from the straw. While Pa unloaded the first wagon full of oats bundles, we usually had two work crews go out with a tractor and wagon to load more bundles of oats.

By age nine or ten, all of us children, boys and girls, had to learn how to use a pitchfork to load the oats bundles onto the wagons. The wagons had open sides, so we had to load the bundles in such a way that we built a wall on each side. That meant we had to put the stubble end of the oats bundles on the outside. The top of each bundle where the oats were located was the heaviest end. Therefore, we would make one row of bundles with the straw end on the outside and the heavy oats end on the inside, throwing a bunch of other bundles on top to hold them down. We continued to repeat the whole process until the wagons were full and ready to be unloaded.

Then we all jumped onto the tractor and brought the load in to where the thresher was located. The goal was to get another full load to Pa by the time he was finished unloading the previous wagon of oats. We could usually see from a distance how close Pa was to getting his wagon unloaded, so the pressure was on. Sometimes, we had to drive the tractor at high speeds to get the next wagon load of oats bundles to Pa in time.

If the outside walls of the loaded wagons were not built stable enough, on both sides, we ran the risk of losing the entire load of oats—dumping them all over the field. That seldom happened because most of us children were amazingly well-trained and dependable little slaves. When it did happen, Pa was furious because that meant lost time.

As long as we had two work crews loading wagons, we could usually keep up with no problem. However, if we had only one work crew loading wagons, we had to load the wagon really fast to keep up.

Sometimes, I had the job of using a pitchfork to help load the wagon, and other times I had to drive the tractor while my brothers loaded the wagon. The most difficult part of driving the tractor was putting the clutch down to stop the tractor in the middle of a steep hill while my brothers were loading the wagon. I was such a lightweight girl that I had to put all of my weight on the tractor clutch to get it to go down.

Once when I was on an extra steep hill, one brother yelled stop at the same time the other one yelled, "Go—let it go!" I didn't know what to do until I glanced back and realized that the wagon had jackknifed and was coming very close to flipping over on top of me. I immediately let it go all the way down to the bottom of the hill. I probably would have been killed or paralyzed if I had made the wrong split-second choice.

A full wagon load of oats rose up to at least eight feet or more from the ground, so we needed to use long-handled pitchforks to stack bundles that high. Unfortunately, while loading the wagons, there was always the risk of a pitchfork getting caught under the wagon and breaking, especially if the tractor driver thought all the loaders were done and began moving forward too soon. That's exactly what happened to Pa's shiny, brand-new pitchfork when I was using it. Pa always kept track of how many pitchforks he had, too, and I was afraid he would give me a whipping.

Luckily, my brother Bernie came to my rescue. He said he knew where another pitchfork handle was, and he could fix it before Pa found out. So we hid the broken pitchfork in a shock and marked the location so he could sneak back into the field to replace the broken handle later that night. What Bernie did not tell me is where he found the other pitchfork handle. It was in the barnyard with all kinds of dried-up, baked-on manure all over it.

That night, Bernie climbed out of the upstairs window, jumped from the house roof down onto the roof of our garage, and climbed down the ladder that he had previously set up. Then he took the old pitchfork handle out to the field to replace the new broken handle.

While Bernie was gone, Pa called upstairs to him, "Bernie, did you remember to feed more corn to the hogs?" Trying to sound like my brother, I yelled down in a low voice, "Yeah!"

Pa said, "Good" and never discovered that Bernie was not there.

When Bernie returned, I told him what Pa asked, and Bernie said, "Oh no! I forgot to do that, so I better sneak back out and do it now."

The next day when we brought a full load of oats bundles in to the thresher, we pulled out Pa's empty wagon and pulled in our full wagon. Pa always left his pitchfork on his empty wagon, and we always left one of our pitchforks on the full wagon for Pa.

I did not know until later that Bernie purposely left the shitty pitchfork handle on Pa's wagon. At the supper table, Pa said, "I don't remember any of our pitchforks having manure all over the handle. Whatever happened to the one with the brand-new handle?"

Luckily, Pa did not pursue it further. He still had the right number of pitchforks, so that really baffled him.

The worst part of loading the wagons was that field mice and garter snakes often made their homes in the stubble of the oats bundles. Frequently, when we lifted the bundles with our pitchforks, the field mice would scurry all over the place, and sometimes they ran up our pant legs. When that happened, I simply shook them out, jabbed them in the belly with my pitchfork, and put them in the toolbox of the tractor to feed to our cats when we got home.

What really freaked me out were the garter snakes. Even though garter snakes are harmless, snakes of any and every kind have always terrified me. Most of the time the snakes in the oats bundles just slithered away as soon as I tipped the bundle over, and that alone was bad enough to startle me and give me some jitters.

One day, I was in the process of placing the last oats bundle on top of a full load. Just as I had the handle of my pitchfork extended directly over my head, an entire family of garter snakes came showering down on top of me from inside the stubble of the oats bundle. A couple of them even fell into my blouse. I immediately dropped my pitchfork and did a wild witch dance in the field, yelling and screaming bloody murder as I shook them out of my blouse.

At first, my brothers didn't know what happened. They must have thought I was suddenly possessed by the devil. That was an awful experience. To this day, I am deathly afraid of any and all snakes.

Sometimes, we would get a chance to dig a tunnel in one side of the straw piles, crawl in, and take a brief nap. When my brother Buzz was about seven years old, he dug a tunnel in the side of a straw pile while the threshing machine was still running and adding more straw. After Buzz crawled in, he fell asleep. By the time he woke up, he could no longer see the entrance to his tunnel because it had been covered up with more fresh straw. When Buzz dug his way out again, it was already dark, and the entire threshing crew had gone home. Poor little Buzz had to find his way home in the dark. Apparently, nobody missed him at the supper table. That's how it is in a large family; it's easy to overlook one or two if parents don't take roll call.

BALING STRAW

Baling straw was fairly easy when the job was done while the straw pile was fresh, dry, and fluffy; sometimes, though, Pa waited until late in the fall, after we had our first freeze or two, and the straw was packed under layers of ice. Once Pa brought the hay baler out to the field to bale straw, and several of us children had to climb up onto the frozen straw pile to help pry up the ice and shove the dry straw down to the bottom. As a young girl of about ten years old, I did my best to pry up those layers of ice, but I was not able to do it as quickly as Pa expected. Every once in a while, when Pa wanted me to work faster, he used his pitchfork to jab me in my legs. I feel lucky my legs did not get any permanent damage.

ROTTEN POTATOES

Have you ever smelled a rotten potato? The odor is overpowering, whether it's a small bag of potatoes or even just one. So imagine a huge pile of rotten potatoes that filled an entire room from the floor to the ceiling. Add to it the smell of the sewage water that caused the potatoes to rot in the first place. No words are strong enough to describe the smell.

Every year, we harvested a large crop of potatoes that were dumped onto gunnysacks on the basement floor—enough to feed a big family all year round. As long as the floor stayed dry, the cold basement kept the potatoes well preserved until they were gone. However, one year we had a clogged sewer, and the sewage water backed up far enough to reach the pile of potatoes on the other side of the room. The smell was absolutely putrid. Somebody had to clean it up, and guess who that somebody was? Me.

As a twelve-year-old, every day after school I had to endure that horrible stench and use a shovel to scoop the rotten potatoes into a bucket. Then I had to carry one bucketful at a time up a flight of stairs and dump it outside—far enough away that the smell did not come back into the house. For a young girl, carrying heavy buckets of potatoes up a flight of stairs was a strenuous job. Every day after school, I worked for several hours, but it still took me at least a month to get it all cleaned up. That, my friends, was the most toilsome indoor job I ever had to do.

No wonder I developed such big trucker-arms and could out arm wrestle most of the boys at school.

*Pa frequently lectured us about fire safety
and prevention, and he severely punished Buzz
for playing with matches.*

*Threshing season was like a punishment to us because shocking
oats and loading wagons with oats bundles was one of the most
difficult jobs we had to do every summer. Pa had Oliver tractors
with two little wheels in front.*

PUNISHMENTS
OF AN
UNUSUAL KIND

MY SIBLINGS AND I were surprisingly well behaved. We didn't smoke cigarettes, never used drugs, never got drunk, and never broke the law. At least, none of us older children did any of those things, and if any of my younger siblings did, I never heard about it. We were obedient and did all of the jobs our parents asked us to do, whether we liked it or not. We mostly just got punished for not working hard enough, fast enough, or well enough to please Pa.

NO BED-WETTING

Pa often cracked down on us kids for bed-wetting, but the main reason it was a problem is because he scared the piss out of us. Pa never had a clue what caused children to wet the bed in the first place, and he had no idea how to solve the problem. He only made it worse.

Pa's solution was to spank us or make us sleep outside on some hay in the cold barn with the animals, which only increased our stress. Spanking might have worked, if any of us were lying in bed awake and deliberately wetting all over ourselves. I have yet to know of any child who would do such a thing. Making us sleep in the barn on some hay did not work either. The only good that did was to give some of us firsthand experience of what it was like for the baby Jesus to sleep in a manger.

I talked with a doctor fifty years ago about what causes children to wet the bed. I don't remember his name, but I was surprised any of us children ever slept dry after I heard what he had to say:

- Children who are constantly living under a lot of stress and duress are far more likely to wet the bed. Strike One: We were definitely victims of stress overload.

- Children who overwork their bladders during the day make it nearly impossible for their bladders to work for them at night. On the other hand, children who go to the bathroom at least six times a day should not have a problem. Strike two: We didn't have access to bathrooms during the day when we were working in the fields, so we often held it until we got home.

- Children who do not drink enough fluids during the day are far more likely to wet the bed. Strike Three: We often did not have enough to drink during the day when working in the fields. By the time we got home, we were often so thirsty we drank half a gallon of water just before going to bed.

- Children who work extra hard might be too tired to wake up to use the bathroom during the night. Strike Four: We were definitely victims of that, also.

NO BATHROOM IN CHURCH

The Sacred Heart Catholic Church had a bathroom in the basement, but none of us children were allowed to use it during Sunday Mass, no matter how badly the urge arose. Having a dozen children in the same house to share only one bathroom, however, often made it impossible for all twelve of us to use it beforehand.

As unrealistic as it was, Pa insisted that we all use the bathroom before church so we would not have to get out of the pew and go during the church service. If Pa saw any of us children leave during Mass to use the bathroom, that kid would get severely punished when we returned home.

Below is what my brother Mark had to say about it:

> *The trouble is that he (Pa) forgot what it was like being a kid. You simply didn't go to the bathroom until your water tank was full, and with such wonderfully working bladders as a kid has, when it did get full, you absolutely had to unload it now. This made for a choice between getting a beating after church or wetting your pants and hoping the Old Man didn't notice until after you got home to change the britches. As bad as the beatings were, the choice was always easy—pee in the pants and hope not to get caught.*
>
> *One Sunday one of the smaller boys had this exact situation occur. It was during a sermon,*

*very quiet as usual, and the whole congregation
was introduced to the sound of running water in
the middle of the church somewhere. Even the
preacher looked in our direction.*

*Now I can attest to the fact that when a young
bladder suddenly lets go, there is no stopping it
until you are done. We were so glad that the Old
Man was hard of hearing from all of the loud
tractors and machinery. He didn't have a clue
what was going on, but I knew very well and
why. I think my little brother was trying to keep
his pants dry by peeing directly on the vinyl floor.
It was very easy to do on your knees with the
pew backs up to your chin—just whip it out and
let it fly underneath the pew in front of you, or
if you could wait until you were standing up, it
would be safer because of singing or response. It
was harder to hear, and one could run most of it
down their pant leg.*

NO FIGHTING ALLOWED

Pa had some awfully strange ideas about discipline. He figured
it was reasonable to have more than a dozen children living
under one roof and expect them to never have fights. How
unrealistic is that? Sibling squabbles are common, something
most parents expect. Realistic or not, one day when I was ten
years old, Pa decided we kids were fighting too much, and he
came up with a perfect solution to make us stop.

Pa announced that the next time he caught any of us kids
fighting, he would decide whose fault it was, and we would
learn a lesson we would never forget. Pa had a plan to make

it work. The next time there was an open casket viewing at the local funeral home, whoever started fighting with another sibling would have to look at the dead person close up and imagine it was the brother or sister with whom we were fighting.

Not long after Pa told us that, he walked into the house just as my sister Rose threw a shoe at me. I happened to be standing in front of the dining room window. I ducked, and the shoe went through the window. Pa immediately decided it was my fault the window got broken, because I should have let the shoe hit me instead. I certainly did not believe that was fair because Rose started the fight, and she was the one who threw the shoe. But Pa's mind was made up, so I was the first (and maybe the last) one who had to go to the funeral home and look at a dead person close up.

"Now imagine that's the sister you were fighting with lying there," Pa said as he forced me to look at the old dead man. As a ten-year-old, I was not ready to see a dead body. It scared me so much that I can still remember the dead man's name and what he looked like. For several years after that, I had nightmares that Rose was dead and it was my fault.

Pa's cure for sibling rivalry and squabbles was a complete failure, but he was right about one thing: It was something I never forgot. All it did, however, was guarantee that I would never be able to have a close relationship with my sister Rose. Every time I see her, all I can think about is that horrible experience.

KNIFE TRAUMA

When I was eleven years old, Pa handed me a cheaply made corn knife in late summer. He then ordered me to go out into the cornfield to cut down two rows of corn by hand.

"I want you to go to the far end of the cornfield, count four rows in from the lane, chop down the corn stalks in rows five and six, and lay them down in row seven," Pa said. "I want you to cut those two rows of corn stalks down all the way to the end. You better be quick about it, too, because I am coming out there with a tractor and trailer pretty soon to pick it up, and if I catch up to you, I will give you a licking you will never forget."

The single-lane dirt roadway cut through the middle of our fields with an electric, barbed wire fence on each side. I knew this would be no easy job because those rows of corn appeared to be at least a mile long. I ran out to the field and started chopping the corn stalks down as fast as I could. At first I felt like I was making really good progress. The sun was shining, but it wasn't too hot, and I did not mind doing hard work as long as I could avoid one of Pa's whippings. Unfortunately, the flimsy corn knife Pa gave me soon started to bend and break in the middle. At first, I just bent it back straight again, but it never lasted very long, and I was afraid it would soon break in half. Having to stop to bend the knife back in place every few minutes was slowing me down, and it put me in a really bad dilemma.

If I went back to get it fixed, I would lose too much time. On the other hand, I feared that if I did not do something to get the knife fixed, it might break, and then I would also be in serious trouble. Reluctantly, I made the decision to run back to find one of my brothers to solder it back together. As I was looking for my brother to get the knife fixed, Pa came out the back door of our farmhouse.

"What the hell are you doing still here when you are supposed to be out in the field cutting down that corn?" he yelled as soon as he saw me.

"I was cutting the corn, but look, the corn knife started breaking," I said. "I came back to get it fixed."

"Let me see that damn knife!" Pa said.

I handed it to him, and then he did the same thing I had already done. He simply bent it back straight and handed it back to me.

"There. Now I fixed it, so get back out there and cut down that corn!" Pa said. "You better hurry because I will be there pretty soon."

My heart sank as I realized I wasted too much time to get the knife repaired, and now I would have to try to finish the job with a corn knife that was still breaking. No way could I cut down the corn stalks very quickly. I knew the knife would surely break if I whacked away at the corn stalks like I did at first. I would have to slow down and cut the corn stalks very carefully so I would not break the knife.

Soon, I heard the awful sound of the tractor and trailer approaching. As I watched out of the corner of my eye, I saw Pa approach closer and closer. I knew I would not be able to stay ahead of him. Soon, he started yelling at me to cut the corn faster and faster, but I was already doing the best I could without breaking the knife. When Pa caught up to me, he was awfully angry.

"But the knife will break if I cut any faster," I said.

"Here, give me that damn knife, and I'll show you how to do it!"

Pa grabbed the knife from my hand and swung hard—whack! On his very first swing at the corn stalks, the corn knife snapped, and the broken end went flying into the air.

"Now look what you made me do!" Pa hollered.

Pa was furious; he threw me into the dirt and used the

remaining part of the corn knife to whip me. I thought for sure I was going to die right there in the cornfield, and he would probably just dig a hole and throw me in.

Finally, Pa dropped the knife, rubbed my face in the dirt, kicked me in the butt, and said, "Now get the hell out of here before I kill you!"

I always knew Pa was capable of killing me, and that day, in that moment, he knew it, too, because he even said it out loud.

When I got back to the house, tattered, dirty, bloodied, and battered, Ma did not even ask me what happened. I cleaned myself up as well as I could and cried myself to sleep, dreaming about the day I could leave and never return.

That day I swore to myself that if I ever lived long enough to grow up and leave, I would never make the same mistake as Pa. I would never buy cheap, flimsy tools or appliances that break so easily. I would wait and save my money until I could purchase only top-quality items that I could depend on—and I did, too. I buy only dependable cars, washers, dryers, refrigerators, and stoves. I buy quality, or I do not buy at all—and it is all Pa's fault, too.

MOLDY BREAD

Ma baked six loaves of bread and two pans of rolls every other day. Whenever Ma needed more time to finish doing the laundry or something else, she would burn the bread on purpose so that we would not eat it so quickly. Then she would be able to wait another day before she had to make more. By doing that, however, Ma created a major problem.

All of the bread was kept in a bread drawer. When Ma burned the bread, all of us kids would eat the middle out of the bread and throw the burned bread crust back into the drawer. Every once in a while, Pa would open the bread drawer and find all of the wasted pieces of bread crust, and that made Pa very angry. When I was about twelve, Pa gathered us kids together and held up a pan full of wasted bread crusts that were so old they already had green mold on them.

"Who did this?" Pa asked. "Which one of you kids did this?"

Of course, that was a ridiculous and illogical question because we all did it. Because we all did it, none of us wanted to claim responsibility for the entire amount. Like officers in charge of basic training in the military, Pa was very much into group punishment. Therefore, Pa handed us the pan of moldy bread, locked us in the basement, and said he would not let us out until we did one of two things: tell him who did it, or eat it until it was completely gone.

Of course, none of us wanted to eat the moldy bread, and none of us wanted to take the blame for what we all did, so we started to have a discussion about who might be punished the least, if we made a deal for one of us to take the responsibility. Then we heard a noise coming from under the stairs. It was our dog, who was stuck down there with us. That's when we got the great idea to get our dog to eat the bread for us. We could tell he did not want to eat it any more than we did, but I guess he was hungry enough to do it anyway.

About a week later, our dog got very sick, most likely from eating that moldy bread, and we were glad we did not eat it ourselves. At least our good and faithful dog saved us from getting sick. Pa definitely put our health in grave danger by trying to force us to eat moldy bread.

ANIMAL TORTURE

Pa had a cow named Roberta that frequently broke through his fences, and then other cows would follow. Finally, Pa got sick and tired of having to chase his cows down and continuously repair broken fences.

I was about fourteen years old when Pa told me to get into his station wagon because he needed my help to find Roberta in the pasture and chase the cow into the lane. The lane had an electric barbed wire fence on each side of a single-lane dirt road. Once we got Roberta into the lane, Pa drove the station wagon into the lane, and the cow was trapped with nowhere to go except straight ahead.

As I rode in the backseat of the station wagon, I soon learned that Pa was on a mission of vengeance.

Pa said he decided to kill the cow, but first he was going to punish her for all the trouble she put him through. Pa chased the cow down the lane with the car directly behind her, forcing Roberta to run faster and faster. At the same time, Pa had a shotgun and started shooting buckshot at the cow's rump. I never saw a cow run that fast for so long, and I watched in disbelief as Roberta's utter swung back and forth. The poor animal frequently turned her head to look back, and she had such a desperate look on her face. I wanted Pa to stop tormenting that poor animal, but Pa was not about to stop. He was actually enjoying it. The more anguish the cow went through, the more Pa laughed.

"This will teach that stupid cow a lesson," he said, as he unloaded more buckshot.

Pa continued to drive his car faster and faster until the cow could run no longer. Finally, the cow got so exhausted it stumbled and dropped to the ground.

A few of my brothers doubted that Pa would have done such a thing, but they were not there. I was there, and I can still see the image of that cow's tortured face as clearly as if it happened yesterday.

FIRE BY THE SEAT OF THE PANTS

When my brother Buzz was young, he often got caught playing with matches. Pa admitted in his autobiography that he, himself, was a firebug when he was a kid. Just like Buzz, he had a fascination with fire. That's why Pa was so worried about the farm catching on fire, so he did not want to take any chances of any of us turning into firebugs.

I watched as Pa tried to discourage Buzz from playing with fire by forcing him to hold a burning matchstick. Pa didn't allow him to let go until it burned all the way down to his fingers. When that didn't work, Buzz said Pa turned on the gas stove and held his hands in the fire. Even that, however, did not seem to discourage Buzz from playing with matches.

Finally, Pa decided to give Buzz a fire so big that he would never want to play with fire again. Pa handed Buzz a gunnysack, took him out to the field, and set a huge old straw pile on fire. The straw pile was surrounded by six-inch-high dry oats stubble.

"It was a windy day," Buzz said. "I was supposed to keep the fire from torching the whole field and spreading to other fields."

Pa ordered Buzz to stay out there and fight the fire with the gunnysack until all of the straw burned to the ground and the fire was completely out. That meant Buzz had to fight the fire for several hours.

I was the first one to see Buzz when he finally came home late that night. He was a sight to behold. He looked completely exhausted, but not defeated. He was black from ashes and soot from head to foot. In fact, he looked very much like the Tar Baby in the *Brer Rabbit and the Tar Baby* storybook.

I took just one look at him and asked, "Well, did you enjoy the fire?"

The "Tar Baby" smiled, showing his white teeth, and his eyes twinkled.

"It was hard, but I did my job," Buzz said. "You should have seen it. The flames shot so high I thought they were going to scorch the clouds."

Uh-oh, I thought, *Buzz is not done playing with fire yet.*

Not long after that, when I was fifteen years old, I was left at home in charge of babysitting my younger siblings, and I caught Buzz trying to sneak a box of wood matches outside. I grabbed them away from him and chased him outside. Then I hid them on the top shelf in the cupboard behind other items where he could not see them. What I did not know was that Buzz was peeking through the kitchen window and saw where I hid them. As soon as I went into another room, Buzz came back in and got the matches.

Somehow, he talked our brothers Matt and Paul into playing a game I'll call "Fire by the Seat of the Pants." Here's how it worked:

They would take turns lighting the seat of each other's pants on fire and see who dared to let it burn the longest before sitting down to put the fire out. They were not worried about ruining their work britches because they were already so ragged they didn't care if they put a few extra burn holes in them. To get the pants to burn, they decided to put a few sprinkles of gasoline on them. Buzz and Matt were old enough to know, however, that using gasoline might be a little risky. Unbeknownst to them, in Paul's effort to emulate his older brothers, he put far more than a few drops of gasoline on the back of his pants.

As soon as Paul's pants were lit, flames shot up so high he got scared and did the absolute worst thing he could do. He took off running so fast that his big brother Mark had a hard time catching him to roll him on the ground and put the fire out.

"Mark saved my life," Paul said. "I'm glad he was there because he was the one who caught me and put the fire out."

Afterward, Buzz and Matt took Paul to the cow watering tank to cool his burns down, but Paul was already burned badly enough to get bubble blisters all over his back.

Buzz and Matt knew that if Pa found out, they would be severely beaten. To ensure that Pa did not know, Buzz and Matt did all of Paul's chores for the next several weeks until he recovered. They knew that as long as all of Paul's work got done, Pa would never miss him and never know.

"I think Ma did find out, but Mark is the one who was changing my bandages," Paul said. "It left a scar on my back that's still there."

Seeing his little brother go up in flames like a human torch scared Buzz so badly that he never played with fire again.

NO SCHOOL DANCE

Ma seldom hit us or spanked us, but she never stopped Pa from doing it. A few times she even contributed to it or encouraged it.

When I was sixteen years old, I thought it might be fun to

attend a free school dance, so I nicely asked Ma if I could go. That was a big mistake. Ma went crazy, and I was shocked at her reaction.

"Sure, you can go to a school dance," she said. "Go ahead. Meet a boy, pull your pants down, and get pregnant out of wedlock. See if I care!"

Ma's response made no sense. I didn't even have a boyfriend. The only reason I asked if I could attend the school dance was to socialize because my girlfriends wanted me to be there. After Ma's reaction, however, I just dropped it and decided not to go. But Ma did not drop it.

Later that evening, when I was upstairs doing my school homework, Ma told Pa that I wanted to attend the school dance. The two of them had a big discussion of what they thought could happen if I went. Before long, they blew it way out of proportion. It was totally unreal.

"In fact, I am so sure that Barbara is going to get pregnant out of wedlock that I am going to punish her for it right now," Pa said.

I had never even been on a date, but Pa came upstairs, grabbed me, dragged me downstairs, and gave me a heck of a beating right in front of Ma—all for what they thought I might do.

After I already received a beating for what my parents thought I was going to do, I would have had every right to go out and do it, but then they would have felt justified for punishing me ahead of time. Instead, I was all the more determined to prove to them how wrong they were. I wanted to look them in the eyes and say, "Shame on you for wrongly punishing me for something I never did."

I was a very pretty young lady at that age, but I didn't

know it. None of the boys at school ever showed any interest in me. Perhaps they heard rumors about what a tyrant Pa was, and they were too afraid to even think of dating any of Pa's daughters.

People used to make a big deal out of being "sweet sixteen and never been kissed." Well, I was sweet sixteen, seventeen, eighteen, and nineteen and still had not been kissed. I didn't even go on my first date until I was nineteen. After changing diapers on my younger siblings, I was in no hurry.

When I moved to Tacoma, Washington, to get away from the cold Minnesota weather, I met plenty of young men who were stationed at the local Army post and Air Force base, but I knew how to conduct myself.

When I applied for a job at Richards Commercial Photography Studio, during my interview the boss man said, "With your Gregg stenography skills to take dictation and your ability to type 100 words per minute, you certainly have more than enough qualifications to do this job, but you are such a pretty young lady, you might only be here for a few short weeks before you get pregnant and run off with some young man."

In the late 1960s, bosses could say just about anything during a job interview. They would never get away with saying anything like that now.

"I'm not that kind of girl," I said. "In fact, before going on dates, I always grease my neck down with Vicks VapoRub, and that discourages all of them from getting too fresh. None of my dates want to get a mouth full of Vicks VapoRub. It works really well."

The boss man liked my response. I got hired, and I worked there for more than a year.

UNFAIR BEATINGS

When I was about eighteen, I heard a ruckus outside, and I ran over to the window to see what was happening. Pa was beating three of my younger brothers, banging their heads against the concrete part of the barn wall and hitting them with a board. Ma was looking out the window, too.

"Mom, make him stop," I pleaded. "Please make the Old Man stop. I think he's killing them!" But Ma just stood there, shaking and trembling like a scared child herself.

I hated to see any of my siblings get beaten, and I seldom knew what they did to make Pa so angry. I just knew none of us deserved the horrible beatings we received. We rarely did anything wrong, but Pa always found reasons to punish us anyway. My brother Buzz shared what happened to him:

> When I was twelve, I was in the trees when my brother (Matt) came running over to tell me the Old Man wanted me in the barn. I went. He grabbed me and said I had given the calves too much grain. It didn't make them sick, and he never told us the right amount to feed them. 'No matter,' he said. 'You are no damned good and will never amount to anything.' Then he commenced a vicious beating. After many blows from the 180-pound enraged devil, my 90-pound body collapsed in the foot-deep manure. After kicking me a few times, he told me to get up so he could beat me some more. I just lay in the shit glaring at him with eyes that conveyed the betrayal I felt from someone who was supposed to love me.

Pa then went to the house and told Ma to get Buzz and clean him up.

One thing is for sure, Pa could not have been more wrong about Buzz. The boy he said would be "no damned good" ended up graduating from the University of St. Thomas. Buzz became a teacher, earned a master's degree in business education, and owns a successful house painting business.

I am very proud of all of my siblings for all they have been able to do with their lives.

*The three children I babysat when I was in high school—
Tim, Ruth, and Kathy, with a drawing of their puppy Cindy.*

YOUNG ENTREPRENEURS

UNLIKE MANY OF OUR CLASSMATES, my siblings and I never got paid an allowance for doing chores. We were expected to earn our room and board.

Pa never gave us anything for free. In fact, even when it came to his will—the last chance he had to give anything to anyone—he put a price tag on that, too.

Pa sent me a letter, which I still have, stipulating what we children needed to do to receive an inheritance. For a full year prior to his death, we would have to prove that we attended church every Sunday and regularly tithed.

Of course, we had no idea when Pa was going to die, so he must have thought he had us over a barrel. Yet he received enough money from his grandmother to buy his first farm, and he never had to do anything to get it, either.

I felt safe telling Pa what I thought of his inheritance letter because I lived 2,000 miles away. In a letter I wrote back to him, I said, "If any of us went to church just to qualify to get your inheritance money, we would not be there for the right reason. Trying to buy our way into Heaven is wrong. Setting a good example would do more for our religious attitude than all the inheritance money in the world."

At the end, I suggested Pa could start by not getting angry about my letter. Later, my heart sank when I learned that Pa gave my sweet little sister Missy a horrible beating just because she agreed with what I wrote in my letter. Pa threw her across the room, and Missy wrote and begged me not to send any more letters like that. Many of my siblings agreed with what I had to say, so Pa punished us by taking everyone out of his will except for two siblings and Ma.

Pa was a tightwad, and he never learned how to give anything to anyone out of love, except maybe Tom. He helped his firstborn son purchase a farm that was located about seventeen miles from our farm. Bottom line: If any of us children wanted or needed anything, we had to figure out creative ways to earn the money ourselves. Sometimes we had to skip hot lunch at school and go hungry to buy school supplies instead. None of us were lazy, however, so we usually found ways to make money.

EARLY BABYSITTING EXPERIENCE

I got a lot of babysitting experience at a very young age, but I never got paid for babysitting my younger siblings. My parents often left me at home to babysit younger siblings, including infants, when I was just a child myself. By the time I was six years old, I already knew how to change diapers and fix baby bottles.

Once all of my older brothers and sisters had already received their first Holy Communion in second grade, they started going to confession every six weeks with my parents. As the oldest one who had not yet made my first Holy Communion, I was the one who had to stay home and babysit all of my younger siblings. In other words, I was only in first grade when I was left in charge of five younger siblings, including an infant.

Once when I was left at home to babysit, Ma forgot she had bread baking in the oven. I didn't discover it until after they left. The oven burner was broken, and I knew Ma used a special gadget to turn the burner off, but I did not know where it was or how to use it. I was in a panic. I knew by the time my parents got home, the bread would be burned, and I would be in trouble.

I decided to try to telephone the church, which was no easy task in those days. We had a huge, box wall phone with a crank on it. Our telephone number was two long rings and a short. I had no idea how to call the church, but I got lucky because we were on a party line. When I attempted to call, Florence Andert, our neighbor, heard me and asked what was wrong. Luckily, she knew about the special gadget Ma used, so she was able to tell me where to find it and how to use it. With her help, I was able to get the oven turned off before the bread burned.

It was a good thing, too, because that night my parents decided to go to an outdoor movie after church, and they didn't return home until really late.

One of my younger siblings started crying, then another, and another, and another. The only one not crying was me. I could not make any of them stop crying, and I didn't know what to do. I put all of them in Ma and Pa's bed and tried to sing them to sleep. But they still wouldn't stop crying, so I started crying, too. When I started crying, the rest of them finally shut up, and we all went to sleep.

CORN PICKING

When I was ten, some of my older siblings and I made a little money by walking through our cornfields to find and pick up corn that our corn picker missed.

Every night after school, we took gunnysacks to the corn-field, filled them with the corn we found, and dragged our bags of corn home. After we weighed our bags and recorded how much we each got, we dumped our corn into a small wagon about the size of a U-Haul trailer. Minnesota weather got cold in the fall, and I seldom had mittens, so it was cold, miserable work. Finally, when we had a wagon full, we climbed onto the tractor to pull the wagon to the mill to sell our corn and then collect our money. For a whole month's work, I earned only $5.27, but that was about the most mon-ey I ever had at that age.

TRAPPING GOPHERS

To us kids, trapping gophers seemed like a logical thing to do. Minnesota is, after all, the "Gopher State." We had plenty of gophers on our farm. They were destructive to our crops, so we older children often trapped them, cut their feet off, and took the feet to the agriculture office at the courthouse in town as proof of how many gophers we had killed.

It was an awful lot of work. It didn't pay well, but when we had no money at all, every little bit helped.

The striped gopher feet were worth only 5 cents, but the

pocket gopher feet were worth 25 cents each, so we mostly tried to catch pocket gophers, which caused more destruction to the crops than the striped gophers.

Whenever we found a gopher hole, we knew there had to be another hole nearby. To ensure the gophers did not go down one hole and escape out the other one, we always found both holes before we tried to catch the gophers. After we plugged one hole, we got several buckets of water and poured them into the open hole, giving the gophers a no-win situation—either come out or drown.

Buzz learned the hard way that the last thing he should do was to attempt to grab a gopher with his bare hands as soon as it poked its head out of the hole. One time, Buzz shoved his hand down the hole to grab the gopher, and it bit down on his fingers, refusing to let go. Several of us beat and jabbed the gopher for a long time before it finally dropped to the ground and set my brother free.

The gophers usually came out when we poured the water into the hole. When they did, about four or five of us kids were waiting with pitchforks and stones in hand. The gophers didn't have a chance. As they scampered in all directions, and we tried to jab them with our pitchforks, it was truly amazing that we never accidentally stabbed each other in the foot.

Later on, Mark said most of the time they would shoot the gophers with the 22 rifle, and they got fourteen of them in one Sunday afternoon.

DRAWING CARTOONS

One of my first jobs was getting paid by a classmate's mother to draw life-size images of Fred and Wilma Flintstone with

Barney and Betty Rubble on the walls in their recreation room.

I also entered drawing contests. I displayed enough natural artistic talent that a representative from the Minneapolis School of Art drove 129 miles to our farmhouse during a Minnesota snow storm to recruit me. Of course, Pa was not about to invest in my artistic training. I often wonder how far I might have gone had I been trained as a graphic artist.

TYPING A BOOK MANUSCRIPT

When I was seventeen, Edward E. Barsness, a retired newspaper editor and former U.S. congressman, stopped by our farm. My parents were gone, so I answered the door, and he introduced himself. When Barsness shook my hand, he said, "My goodness, you are a hardworking young lady. I can tell from the calluses on your hand. I'm writing a book, and I'm looking for a hardworking young lady who knows how to type. Do you type?"

"Yes, I sure do," I said. "I love to type, and I'm very good at it."

In the 1960s, we had to be good at typing because every time we made a mistake, we had to type the entire page over again. Today's technology makes typing so much easier.

"Well, how would you like to do some typing for me on Saturdays at my newspaper office in town?" he asked. "I can't pay much, but I need somebody to type the manuscript for my book, *Europe Calling*."

I took the job. He was right; it didn't pay much. It did pay, however, in other dividends that made the job worth doing. Besides having me type his final book manuscript, Barsness also had me type letters to various bigwigs in Washington,

D.C. He was a brilliant man, and I learned a lot from him. It also gave me job experience and a letter of recommendation I needed later on.

BEST BABYSITTING JOB

When I was in high school, I was sitting in the classroom near the chalkboard when my history teacher, Ronald Skoog, wrote my name along with a few others on the board. I asked him why he did that.

"Because you did not yet pay for your history periodical," he said.

"It's not nice to embarrass me by putting my name on the board," I said. "If I had the money, I would pay for it, but I don't have the money."

"Then why did your sister pay for hers?" he asked.

I told him Ann had a job cleaning house for some old people in town, but I didn't have a job yet.

"Why don't you ask your dad for the money?" he asked.

"Because he always gets angry about every dime he has to spend, and I don't want to disturb the peace in the family," I said.

Then Mr. Skoog erased my name from the chalkboard and asked me to see him after class.

"How would you like a babysitting job?" he asked. "I have three children—Ruth, Tim, and Kathy. I need a babysitter, and I could drive out to your farm to pick you up."

I was thrilled to have a chance to earn a little money, so I quickly agreed.

That was the beginning of the best babysitting job I ever had. It changed my life. Perhaps it even *saved* my life. Over the next few years, the Skoog family became my role model of a healthy, happy, Christian home filled with love.

The Skoogs were not what anyone would call financially wealthy, but they sure had everything else that made a house a home. Some of my classmates at school sometimes referred to Skoog as "the teacher who always carried a Bible under his arm," but I didn't see anything wrong with that. He not only read the Holy Bible, but he also lived it. The entire Skoog family lived it.

The first day I babysat, both parents told me that I was first to read some Bible stories to their children, which they had already marked off. After that, I could read their other favorite storybooks.

I was familiar with Bible stories, but I was a Catholic at the time, and I seldom read from the Bible. It soon became evident that as members of the Baptist church, the Skoog family read a lot from the Bible. When I stumbled trying to pronounce some complicated Biblical names, I felt terribly embarrassed when four-year-old Kathy corrected me.

I enjoyed babysitting for the Skoog children because they were really well-behaved, and the job soon came with other benefits as well. Sometimes they invited me to come early so that I could join them for dinner before Mr. and Mrs. Skoog left for their evening out.

Ethel Skoog was one of the best cooks in town, so every meal was like a feast. Before meals, they always said table grace in their own words. I had never before heard anyone pray from the heart like they did.

Another thing I noticed was how Ron and Ethel Skoog treated each other with so much love and respect. I wished my parents did that. I could tell how much they loved all three of their children, too. I remember thinking how lucky those kids were to live in a home like that. I wanted what they had, and I never forgot that. To this day, I thank God that He gave me the babysitting job for the Skoog children so that family could serve as my role model.

FISHING WORMS FOR SALE

I would honestly have to say the youngest of us fourteen children was the most successful entrepreneur of all, and Joey got started at a very young age, too. When Joey was only four years old, he decided to start a fishing worm business. He did not yet know how to make his own signs, so he got help from us older kids to write "Fishing Worms for Sale" on signs for him to put out by the highway.

Then Joey found several empty cans, put some black dirt in each one, and dug up his own earthworms. He put one dozen worms in some cans and two dozen worms in other cans. Then he kept all of his cans of worms in the basement. Before long, one fisherman after another saw the sign and knocked on our door. Then we yelled, "Joey, you have a customer!"

When little Joey came running to the door, the fishermen were always surprised that such a young boy was the owner of the fishing worm business.

Joey told them how much money he charged per dozen, and he asked how many cans of worms they wanted. Some fishermen would purposely hand Joey $5 or $10, just to see if he could figure out how much change he owed them.

Joey was already a gifted numbers person. He always surprised his customers and the rest of us by knowing the exact change he owed them. In fact, many of his customers were so impressed with Joey's ability to figure it out in his head that they let him keep the change.

Some of us older siblings were jealous because our little brother was raking in the cash. Joey was usually the only one with enough money to go to the convenience store by Lake Amelia to buy popsicles, soda, and candy. I wanted Joey to loan me some money so I could get treats, too, but he charged too much interest.

My brother Buzz told me that he, Matt, and Paul dug 3,000 grub worms out of a manure pile once. They sold them to a resort in town for customers who wanted to go fishing.

TURTLES, MUSKRATS, AND RACCOONS

When Joey was in high school, he earned even more money by selling snapping turtles to restaurants for turtle soup and by trapping muskrats and raccoons. "Back in the 1970s, a muskrat was worth $2.50, and a raccoon was $25 for the fur," he said.

I asked Joey how he used the money. He said he used a lot of it for gas. He was also involved in several high school sports, which usually required extra fees.

MONEY FOR SPORTS

I can attest to the fact that playing high school sports required extra fees, and it was not always easy for some kids to come up with the money. When my brother Mark was in the ninth grade, he told Pa that he wanted to play football and it would cost $9 to rent his uniform.

Pa strongly objected to it.

"No!" Pa said. "If you play football, you will bust up your knees and back. Then you'll be absolutely no darn good to me when it comes to doing farmwork."

Mark had such a deflated look on his face because he wanted to play football in the worst way.

I immediately suspected it was the $9 fee that Pa was most worried about. The rest of us children who were there could not stand to see Mark's desire to play football get shattered so quickly. Therefore, we got together and came up with a brilliant plan.

First, Mark needed $9 to pay the rental fee for his uniform. He already had $1. There were eight of us kids attending school at the time, and we each received $1 per week to pay for our hot lunch. We all agreed to donate our weekly hot lunch money to Mark so he could pay the required fee.

Second, Mark needed to have a permission slip signed by one of our parents, giving him permission to play. I was usually the go-to person whenever any of my siblings needed a school note. It was easy for me to duplicate Ma's handwriting, so I proudly produced the signed permission slip that Mark needed to play football.

Third, Mark needed to have a way to get his chores done on the nights he had football practice, so a few of the other boys agreed to do Mark's chores for him.

Our plan to help Mark realize his dream to play football was brilliant, and it worked. In fact, Mark played football that whole season, and our parents never even knew it. I got a little worried when Mark's picture showed up with his football team in the local newspaper, but Pa never saw it.

Sometimes we children just had to work together to make things happen.

Dr. Gordon Lee came out to our farm and saved my mother's life when she fell down the basement steps. He saved her life more than once. Dr. Lee worked at the local hospital for forty-four years, and in the 1970s, he was the only doctor left in Glenwood for several years. He passed away at age eighty-five in 2010.

Robert Letson, M.D., was Dr. Lee's partner for many years. He was another one of my mother's doctors. He moved to Minneapolis in 1967. Dr. Letson passed away at age eighty-eight in 2015.

NO DOCTORS

WHENEVER ANY OF US GOT SICK or injured, Pa's decision was nearly always the same—no doctors! He controlled all of the money, and he always had the final say about everything. Pa did not want to spend money on doctors, and Ma never dared to question or go against any of Pa's decisions—not even his life-and-death decisions.

Luckily, my siblings and I did not get sick too often, but we did have most of the common childhood ailments. When one got the chicken pox, several of us got the chicken pox. When one got the flu, several of us got the flu. Therefore, Ma often had to take care of multiple sick children at once, and most of the time she was pregnant, too. Staying up half the night tending to sick children could not have been easy, but Ma did what she could.

She gave us aspirin, chicken noodle soup, and hot

homemade honey-and-onion cough syrup and rubbed our congested chests down with Vicks VapoRub or Musterole. I did not mind Vicks VapoRub, and I still use it because I actually like the smell. Musterole was something else. Whenever we were fighting colds with severe chest congestion, it appeared to work miracles on clearing up our congestion so we could breathe better, but it was so strong it felt like it was burning layers of our skin off. Most of the time, those remedies were enough. A few times, they were not.

Two of my sisters, Katherine and Martha, died at home from pneumonia without ever seeing a doctor. Whether or not a doctor could have saved them, I will never know for sure, but I believe they might both still be alive today if they had received professional medical care. Sadly, they were never given a fighting chance to survive. I am going to devote the next chapter to telling their stories.

Pa wrote in his autobiography:

> *The only bad times were when they [the children] were sick. That wasn't so often, but it was a real worry when it happened.*

If this were true, I don't understand why Pa usually put his farmwork first and failed to make us children a priority when we were sick.

One thing I do know is if Ma had not figured out a way to save emergency money for bare essentials she needed to take care of us when we were sick or injured, even more of us might have died at a young age. For example, Ma knew that when Pa returned from the grocery store, he had the habit of removing all of his leftover change from the pockets of his overalls. He always threw it into the top left bureau drawer in our dining room. When Pa was not around, Ma would shake the bureau drawer until some of his change fell down to the ledge below. Pa counted his change sometimes, and other times he did not. When Pa counted his change and questioned where his money went, Ma would always say that maybe it fell onto the ledge below. Then Pa would collect his change and be satisfied. When Pa did not question his missing change for one or two weeks, Ma would collect it and save the money in her purse to buy basic items such as aspirin, cough syrup, VapoRub, and iodine. Ma also bartered with neighbors who stopped by for visits when Pa was not around. She often received money in exchange for a hunk of meat from a butchered hog in our freezer, and she also traded jars of honey in exchange for various items such as cans of coffee. Pa never missed those items.

All of us children received required vaccinations, mostly at school, for diphtheria, tetanus, pertussis (whooping cough), and MMR (measles, mumps, and rubella), but not Dr. Jonas Salk's first polio vaccine (IPV). Pa forbade us to get Salk's polio vaccines because he did not trust them. Most parents were relieved that a cure for the dreaded disease was finally available because prior to that, some children with polio were placed in iron lungs.

My sister Ann disobeyed and got the vaccine to get a free helium balloon. I wanted a helium balloon, too, but I did not dare go against Pa's orders. Later on, I was glad I didn't get the Salk vaccine because it turned out Pa was right. A short time later, the "Salk Polio Vaccine Tragedy" was announced on the radio. Sadly, the process used to inactivate the live virus proved to be defective. In April of 1955, the Salk vaccine, manufactured by Cutter Laboratories, caused 40,000 cases of polio, severely paralyzing 200 children and killing 10. When the liquid or pill form came out, we were allowed to get that.

Other than getting vaccinated, I never saw a doctor before I became an adult. As far as I know, only four of the fourteen children ever saw a doctor—Buzz, Paul, Rose, and Mark.

When Buzz was five years old, he was standing on an inverted five-gallon pail watching Bernie sharpen eight-foot hay mower blades. Buzz lost his balance, and when he fell, he hit his head on the sharp point of a blade that was leaning up on the side of the shed. I was standing outside the shed when it happened, and I remember the panic. While calling out to Ma, Bernie led Buzz to the house, and I saw blood squirting out of the side of his head.

"Dr. Lee came out and slapped a patch on it," Buzz said. "I do not know how much blood I lost, but I could have died."

Indeed, he could have, because Dr. Lee told Ma that Buzz came within a fraction of an inch of hitting a major blood vessel.

"Farming is one of the most dangerous occupations," Buzz said. "I had a classmate die in second grade when a tractor rolled over on him on the side of a hill."

Paul was about five years old when he was standing next to an operating manure spreader in the barnyard and, apparently, nobody noticed him. As most farmers know, it is extremely dangerous to wear loose or baggy clothing around any power-driven machinery, especially while it's operating. As a power-driven shaft rotated along the outside wall of the manure spreader, roller chains on the bed floor inside the spreader moved the manure to the back, where spinning beaters kicked the fertilizer out.

Unfortunately, Paul made the mistake of placing his hand on the rotating shaft that ran along the outside wall of the manure spreader. He was wearing a long-sleeved shirt that got caught in the shaft. As his sleeve wrapped around the shaft, Paul's hand and arm got pulled into the one- to two-inch space between the shaft and the outside wall of the spreader. Luckily, my oldest brother, Tom, saw what was happening and quickly stopped the tractor, shutting down the spreader. By that time, however, Paul was already pinned up to his neck and was literally being strangled to death. When Pa picked up us older kids from Saturday morning catechism at church, he told us what happened. He said, "I got Dr. Lee to come out to the house, but Paul might not make it." The doctor said only time would tell. When we got home, Paul was just lying in bed, and all we could do was pray. After a few days, we knew Paul would survive, but he was about as close to death as he could have been. We all learned a very important lesson. Every day at the dinner table for a long time, Pa lectured us about the dangers of going anywhere near a rotating shaft or conveyor belt.

Unfortunately, Rose always had really bad teeth, and she already had a full set of upper dentures when she was only sixteen. When Rose was ten, she got a bulge about the size of a golf ball that protruded from her throat. At first Pa thought she had the mumps, so Rose stayed home from school for two weeks. When it did not get better, Pa took Rose to the doctor, who said it was from a tooth infection. The doctor cut the puss pocket open, drained the abscess, and put a bandage on it, but he left it open to allow the rest of the abscess to ooze out. When Rose went to school the next day, she said her classmates were afraid to get close to her, but at least she got some medical attention rather quickly.

When Mark was in about sixth grade, he was not so lucky. Before he got treated by a doctor, he went through pure hell.

Many of the livestock on the farm got ringworm, which is highly contagious. Pa did not get a veterinarian to treat them right away. Therefore, when my brothers fed the calves or milked the cows, they soon got ringworm, too. Pa thought all cases of ringworm could be gotten rid of by putting iodine on them. If the ringworm lesions were not very big and on an arm or leg, iodine usually worked. The lesions were gone within a week or two.

Unfortunately, Mark got a ringworm lesion on the side of his head. When it was first discovered, it was still very small, about the size of a sweater button, but the iodine was all gone. By the time Pa finally bought more iodine, Mark's ringworm had already grown so big it covered nearly the entire left side of his head. When Pa started pouring the iodine on Mark's head, it hurt him so badly that Mark screamed out in pain. Some of us kids urged Pa to stop, but he ignored us. Instead of just killing Mark's ringworm, it turned the lesion into a huge bulging pocket of pus. Poor Mark had to attend school and church with that gross-looking abscess on his head. After it got really bad, Pa had to take Mark to a doctor, who drained it, spread a white cream medication on it, and covered it with a bandage. After only one doctor appointment, Ma had to continue the same process at home. Every day for several weeks, Ma had to cut it open to drain the abscess out, put more of the white cream medication on it, and attach a new bandage. And every day for several weeks, Mark had to endure that excruciatingly painful treatment. Even after it healed, Mark's torment was not completely over. It left a visible scar on his head, which he had for a long time. I can only imagine how much courage it took for Mark to face the taunting of classmates throughout his long ordeal.

Such unspeakable physical and emotional torment would be enough to destroy many children for life, but not Mark. I still marvel at the emotional strength and courage he displayed at such a young age.

To this day, I greatly admire Mark for his many outstanding accomplishments, in spite of such horrible childhood experiences. He became a highly decorated warrant officer, and he flew Black Hawk helicopters during Desert Storm. Mark always set high goals for himself, and he still does. Now retired at a beautiful lake home, Mark started competing in running races at age fifty-five, usually 5Ks, and has won more than eighty medals and trophies for gold, silver, and bronze finishes.

LIFE AFTER DEATH

Sometimes Pa's ban on medical treatment extended to Ma, too. When Ma was forty years old, she had her first life-after-death experience.

Ma was carrying some dirty laundry down to our basement to wash in our old-fashioned wringer washing machine. At the top of the basement steps. Ma tripped over some dangling clothes and fell down the full flight of stairs. She managed to get herself back upstairs to her bed, but Ma was six months pregnant at the time. A few minutes later, she miscarried and started to hemorrhage

Pa finished milking cows and came into the house a few minutes later. My oldest sister, Pat, immediately told Pa the bad news.

"Ma fell down the basement steps, and she's bleeding badly," Pat said. "She needs a doctor!"

"Well, I have to read the newspaper first," Pa said. "So get in there and do what you can to stop the bleeding."

Pat was only a young girl of thirteen. She was petrified. I could see the disbelief and panic in her face. For God's sake, Pat had no idea what to do. She hadn't even had a first aid class yet. Somehow, she managed to have enough courage to go back into Ma's bedroom to see what she could do. Later, she recalled the incident:

> I felt terribly afraid that I would be left to raise all of my younger siblings with this father from hell. I somehow felt that if only I'd done more to fulfill whatever my being the oldest sister's duties were, things would have worked out a little better. I guess, like many in the family, I felt that I never measured up to what was expected of me. Yet, it certainly wasn't clear.

Most of us other kids hung around in the kitchen, discussing in hushed voices how worried, scared, and helpless we felt, too. I believe one of my brothers decided to sneak off to the neighbor's house behind Pa's back to call Ma's doctor.

After a few minutes, we saw Pat put our mother's blood-drenched, black fur coat into the bathtub to rinse it out. I wondered how Pa could be just sitting on the sofa, calmly reading the newspaper, while Ma was lying in bed bleeding to death.

What I saw next, I will never forget.

Pat came out to the living room and spoke to Pa in a desperate voice: "I can't stop the bleeding! Ma needs a doctor right now!"

Pa tossed the paper aside, stood up, and slapped Pat across

the face really hard. "I told you I had to finish reading the newspaper first," he yelled. "Now get back in there!"

I felt so sorry for Pat. I just could not believe Pa could be so uncaring and callous toward his own wife and the mother of his children.

A few minutes later, Dr. Gordon Lee showed up, and we children gladly invited him in. Thank God he made house calls! Pa was still sitting on the sofa reading the newspaper, and I saw Dr. Lee give Pa a dirty look, without saying a word. Instead, he went directly into the bedroom to check on Ma. He was in there for a long time. Finally, Dr. Lee came out. The way he glared at Pa, I could tell he wanted to scold Pa with several harsh words, but that was not the time.

He said Ma lost the baby, and it was difficult to stop the bleeding because she hemorrhaged so badly.

"Your wife lost an awful lot of blood, and she is still not in a stable condition," he said. "She needs to go to the hospital right away. We need to move her very carefully, or she could start hemorrhaging again."

Then the doctor ordered Pa to help carry Ma out in a bedsheet, one of them at each end, and carefully place her in the back of his station wagon.

"Any sudden movement could easily cause her to hemorrhage again," he said.

I watched as they carried Ma out in the bedsheet. I felt so relieved and grateful that Dr. Lee took control of the situation.

Pa followed him to the hospital, but we kids waited at home. Very strict visiting age limits were enforced at hospitals in those days.

Later that evening, Pa telephoned from the hospital. Pat answered. Afterward, she called all the rest of us kids together.

"The Old Man said our mother might not make it," Pat said. "You know how awful things would be around here if our mother dies. So we all need to go upstairs and pray for her right now."

About seven of us kids got on our knees around Pat's bed and folded our hands as Pat led us in prayer for God to save our mother's life.

The next day, I was relieved and hopeful to learn that Ma had survived the night. What we did not know until a few weeks later was that Ma had actually died and had come back at the same time we were praying for her. Ma was what they called legally dead. For a short time, she had no pulse or heartbeat.

When Ma recovered and was well enough to come home about two weeks later, I rode along in the car when Pa went to the hospital to bring her home. The first thing Ma did when she got in the car was turn around to thank us kids for praying for her, which really surprised me. None of us were allowed to visit Ma in the hospital, and we never told Pa that we prayed for her. Therefore, I was curious how she knew, especially when she even knew what bed we knelt around.

"How did you know?" I asked.

Ma said when she was in the hospital that first night, she floated out of her body, looked down, and saw the doctors working on her. She saw bright lights and felt like she was floating on clouds. Ma said it was a peaceful feeling, and even though she knew she was passing from this life, she did not want to come back, because she knew she was going to a better place. Suddenly, she was in the midst of a heavenly presence, but she didn't know if it was St. Peter or an angel. She could see us kids praying for her around Pat's bed. When she saw us praying, she was told it wasn't her time yet, and her work on earth was not yet done. Ma was told her children needed her, so she had to go back. The next thing she remembered was waking up in the hospital. But that was only part of her story.

Ma had a rare blood type. The hospital did not have a big enough supply of her blood type, so they had to send for more from St. Cloud, Minnesota, sixty-five miles away. A short time later, a man was in a terrible car accident and was brought to the same hospital. He happened to have the same rare blood type as Ma. The doctors knew they did not have enough blood for both of them, so they basically threw up their hands, with the idea that the one who died first could donate blood to the other one. The man soon died, and the doctors got permission from his family to donate his blood to Ma. According to Ma's story, Pa told the doctors that he did not want Ma to get blood from a black man. Thank God, the doctors ignored him and did it anyway.

Ma remained mentally alert and actively engaged in life for another fifty-three years. Throughout those years, I asked her about her life-after-death experience many times, and her story never changed.

ASIAN FLU PANDEMIC

When I was an Army newspaper reporter, I conducted an interview with a manager who helped track worldwide diseases. His job was to determine what vaccinations soldiers needed before they were deployed overseas.

Just before leaving our meeting, I asked if he happened to have any information about the Asian Flu Pandemic that swept through America in 1957 to 1958.

"Yes, we sure do," he said. "As a matter of fact, I have that chart right here."

I was so surprised when he reached behind his desk and produced a chart showing all of the information I had been curious about for many years.

Looking at the chart, I saw that the official reported death toll of the 1957 Asian Flu Pandemic was about two million, but I later learned it might have been as high as four million. In the United States alone, 69,800 people lost their lives from that flu—mostly young children, senior citizens, and pregnant women.

"I had that flu when I was eleven years old and in fifth grade," I said. "I came very close to becoming part of those statistics because my father refused to take me to a doctor."

"Then you are a living miracle," he said. "Even many children who did see a doctor did not survive."

I was so sick with the Asian flu that I got down to forty pounds and missed half a year of school. Eventually, I could no longer keep food down at all. Whenever I ate anything, I had violent vomiting episodes and even coughed up clumps of blood. At that point, I begged Ma to get a neighbor friend to take me to a doctor.

I know Ma feared I might be dying because she even said it out loud. But she feared Pa even more, and she knew how he hated to take any of us kids to a doctor. He expected Ma to cure whatever illnesses we got with home remedies.

At the time I was near death, Pa was busy outside running an elevator to fill a steel corn crib. Finally, Ma got enough courage to go out and ask Pa if he would take me to a doctor. He was not a bit happy about having to stop his work for even a few minutes to check on a sick child, especially me, the daughter he disliked the most. I could tell, as Pa frequently degraded me at the dinner table in front of my other siblings.

When Pa came into my room, the first thing he did was force a raw onion into my mouth, which made me gag, but he demanded that I swallow it anyway. Pa believed raw onions could cure just about anything. I immediately vomited again and coughed up more clumps of blood.

"You don't need a doctor," Pa yelled. "You took me away from my work for nothing. This is all in your head, and you could get well if you wanted to!"

Then he went back outside to his work—leaving me there to die.

At that moment, I never before had a stronger will to live—to live long enough and become strong enough to one day tell Pa to his face how much I hated him. I prayed that God would at least let me get well enough to do that.

Ma continued to do what she could to take care of me. Eventually I was able to keep some foods down, like Jell-O and chicken noodle soup. The fact that I survived with no doctor or prescription drugs really was a miracle.

After missing half a year of school, I recovered enough to return to my fifth-grade class just two weeks before school was finished for the year, but I still did not have all my strength back. I was so dizzy the schoolroom looked like it was spinning. The teacher handed me a thick stack of missing assignments, but I knew I did not have enough time to finish them in only two weeks.

On some of my better days when I was sick, I could have done some of my school assignments at home. I pleaded with my sister Ann to go to my classroom, get my homework assignments, and give them to me, but she refused.

"It would be way too embarrassing for me to walk into your classroom and ask your teacher for your assignments," she said.

If she would have brought me my homework assignments, I would not have been held back, because I had no failing grades—just incompletes. I begged my teacher to pass me to the next grade because I knew Pa would be terribly angry if I had to repeat a grade. That meant he would have to provide room and board for me for an extra year. Even worse, I would be stuck living under Pa's roof for another year before I could graduate and leave.

My teacher said I could pass if I attended summer school, but I knew Pa would not allow me to attend. I had to help with the farmwork, like weeding the garden, feeding the chickens, and driving the tractor. Farmwork always came before school homework assignments. Many times I didn't have a chance to do my school homework until 10 p.m. I seldom got to bed before midnight, and I often fell asleep on my books.

When Pa discovered I was held back and would have to repeat fifth grade, he came in the house and scolded me because he would have to pay an extra $36 for hot lunch. Of course, if he had taken me to a doctor, I probably could have gotten well sooner, but a doctor would have cost even more money.

When the next school year started, I was not looking forward to repeating fifth grade and sharing the same classmates as Ann. As it was, I missed the first two weeks of school that year, too—not because of illness, but because of an infection I got in my foot from stepping on a rusty nail. Shortly before school started, Ma and Pa were having a terrible argument, and I told some of my brothers and sisters outside that I was going to yell through the open dining room screen window and tell them to "go get a divorce." One of my brothers said, "I dare you!" So I did it.

"Go get a divorce!" I yelled.

"The Old Man is coming after you, and he's going to get you!" Rose said.

Rose lied just to scare me, but I wasn't taking any chances, so I took off running as fast as I could to hide behind our machine shed. I was running so fast that I could not stop when I came upon a pile of boards with a lot of rusty nails sticking up. I tried to leap over them, but instead I landed smack-dab on top of one. The rusty nail went right through my shoe and deep into my right foot. The nail was in so deep that I had a hard time pulling the nail out and getting my shoe off my foot.

Of course, because of Pa's "no doctors" policy, I was afraid to say anything. By the time Ma and Pa found out, my entire foot was so full of infection that it was swollen to double its normal size. Pa took out a syringe with a long needle. It was the same one he used to give tetanus vaccines to his steers and cows. After filling it with the same medication he used on his livestock, he injected it into my foot. Then he ordered Ma to boil water in the big pressure cooker she used for canning food. After the water boiled, Pa shoved my infected foot into the pan of boiling hot water and held it there for what seemed like an eternity. When he finally let me take my foot out, my entire foot was raw red, and the top layers of my skin were actually peeling off. I had to endure several sessions of that torture before the infection was gone and my foot healed enough to get my shoe on again.

My sister Martha, in 1964, six years before she died.

TOO YOUNG
TO DIE

KATHERINE WAS THREE MONTHS OLD and Martha was nineteen years old when they passed away from pneumonia at home without seeing a doctor. This chapter was the most difficult to write, but it is also the main reason I'm writing this book in the first place. By telling Katherine's and Martha's stories for them, I'm attempting to give them a voice as well as some justification that says their lives mattered. Hopefully, their stories will also help others.

KATHERINE'S STORY

Ma gave birth to two non-twin babies in the same year. Rose was born on January 14, 1945, and Katherine was born on December 23, 1945. Sadly, Katherine passed away on March 26, 1946.

I was the sixth born, and Katherine had already passed away about a year before I was born.

In the old days, wakes were often held in the family's own house instead of in a funeral home. A photographer took a photo of baby Katherine lying in her coffin, which apparently was the only photo that was ever taken of her. When I was about four years old, Pat showed me a photo of Katherine lying in her coffin. She was a beautiful baby with naturally curly black hair.

I have no idea what happened to that photo.

When I was in my early twenties and working at a professional photography studio, I did some research and found the name of the photography studio that took Katherine's photo. I wanted to have copies made for all of my brothers and sisters because my younger siblings never saw a photo of her. Sadly, I learned the photography studio that had the negatives had a fire about two years earlier. It appears the negatives were destroyed.

Before Ma passed away, she told me this tragic story about Katherine:

Three-month-old Katherine was sleeping in a buggy next to Ma and Pa's bed. Ma wanted to keep Katherine in her room because it was the warmest room in the house. During the night, Katherine's crying kept waking Pa up. Finally, he became so irritated and angry that he spanked baby Katherine and moved her to the coldest room in the house.

The next morning, Ma noticed Katherine had a fever. Pa was leaving to conduct some business in town. Surprisingly, Ma said Pa asked before leaving if Katherine needed to see a doctor, but Ma did not believe Katherine's fever was too serious. Therefore, Pa left. Soon after Pa left, Katherine's fever quickly got much higher. At that point, Ma knew she needed a doctor, but Ma had no phone and no car. The nearest phone was at the neighbor's farmhouse about two miles away. Ma left Katherine at home with Pat, a two-year-old, and told her to stay there and rock the baby until she got back. She then ran to call a doctor by taking a shortcut through the woods to the neighbor's house. When Ma returned, baby Katherine had already passed away.

I cannot imagine leaving a two-year-old alone in charge of a sick baby. I also suspect that rocking a baby with pneumonia might have done more harm than good, but Ma thought that was her best option.

I have to question why Pa left in the first place, knowing the baby was sick, and then stayed away for so long. He should have at least been concerned enough to hurry back.

MARTHA'S STORY

Martha was born on February 15, 1951. She passed away at home on April 23, 1970, without seeing a doctor. I was a newlywed, age twenty-three, living in Norfolk, Virginia, at the time.

Martha had significant learning disabilities. Ma had German measles when she was pregnant with Martha, and her doctor said that is what caused Martha to be born with Down's syndrome. My parents knew this on the surface; however, they could not accept Martha's intellectual limitations. They were in denial for a long time. They even sent Martha to regular first grade because our school did not have special education classes. Our school did offer kindergarten, but it was only for half days and wasn't mandatory, so only my youngest sister got to attend for two weeks.

Martha was musically gifted and excelled in music. She

could even sing "My Bonnie Lies over the Ocean" in Latin. However, it was very difficult for Martha to attend a regular first-grade class.

I was very protective of Martha, so I always ate my hot lunch quickly so I could go out to the playground at lunchtime to find Martha and look after her.

Eventually, Ma and Pa took Martha out of school and kept her at home. However, they felt obligated to take Martha to church. Martha loved church. Some of my siblings were ashamed of Martha and didn't want to sit by her. They would say, "I don't want to sit by that retard! I don't want anyone to know I'm related to a retard!" It wasn't their fault. Our parents taught them to be ashamed of Martha because they were ashamed of her, and they didn't keep that feeling to themselves. Having a child with a learning disability was perceived as being a threat to their image—a negative reflection of their own intelligence. That's why they never accepted her disability. Even when they were forced to see the truth, they didn't know how to deal with it, and they often blamed each other.

"Think hard now," Pa said. "There must have been some retardation on your side of the family."

"No, no one in my family was ever retarded," Ma said. "I admit there were some alcoholics, but they were intelligent alcoholics."

Then Ma would blame Pa, saying, "There must have been some retardation on your side of the family that you just don't remember."

"No," Pa said. "I admit that we had some womanizers and some crooked politicians on my side of the family, but they were intelligent womanizers and intelligent politicians."

As I listened, I realized Ma and Pa obviously would have

preferred Martha had any problem other than being learning disabled or mentally challenged. I believe mentally challenged would have best described Martha because she was capable of learning.

I felt empathy for Martha and often tried to help her, but Pa made it difficult. Sometimes at the dinner table he said, "To understand a retarded person, you have to be a little retarded yourself," and then he would look directly at me.

I usually sat next to Martha in church anyway, to make sure she didn't do something like throw her mittens into the collection basket. Once after Mass, a lady who was sitting in the pew behind us stopped me on my way out. She smiled and said, "You took such good care of your sister in church, I decided to give this money to you instead of putting it in the collection basket." I was thrilled because I needed some school supplies. Most of all, I wanted to buy some Kleenex tissues so I could wipe my runny nose at school. Sometimes I had no choice but to attempt to wipe my nose with regular school paper because that's all I had.

When Pa heard that the lady in church gave me some money, however, he said, "Good, we can go to the Dairy Queen, and you can use that money to buy everyone an ice cream cone." I felt so angry because they all got dime cones instead of nickel cones, so I had no money left.

When Martha was about ten years old, Ma and Pa heard about a free boarding school about sixty miles away for special needs children that was operated by Catholic nuns. They bought Martha the required new clothes and sent her there. Martha was well taken care of there, but the program closed about a year later because of a lack of funding. I was so disappointed because Martha had several bad cavities, and they were just starting to get her teeth fixed. Pa refused to ever take her to the dentist. A few times Pa took some of us to a really old dentist to get a tooth pulled. I hated to go to that dentist because he shook so badly that I thought the needle would break in my gums, but he was the cheapest one in town. After the Catholic boarding house for learning disabled children closed, Martha just stayed at home.

In many ways, Martha was fairly smart. She could sweep floors, set the table, and wash and dry dishes. When anyone stopped by to visit, Martha knew them by name, and she could carry on a commonsense, normal conversation just like anybody else. Once Pa asked Martha to do a difficult job, and she surprised him and everyone else by saying, "I can't do that because I'm too retarded." Now how smart is that—using her disability as an excuse to get out of doing a difficult job?

Sometimes Pa tried to force Martha to learn things, like how to tell time. She did well on knowing the time on the hour, but when it came to knowing how to tell how many minutes before or after the hour, Martha got confused. When she got the time wrong, Pa held her hands down and used the heavy end of a table knife to pound her knuckles. I still remembered how much that hurt when Pa did it to me. I hated to see Martha get abused like that, so when Pa was not around, I took Martha aside to teach her how to tell time. For me, Martha could get the times correct. However, Pa made her so nervous that she couldn't think straight, so she forgot what she learned.

One day when I was doing dishes with Martha, she asked, "Barb, will the Old Man go to Heaven?"

"I don't think so," I said. "Why do you want to know?"

"Because if he goes to Heaven, I don't want to go there," Martha said. I couldn't help but laugh to know that Martha would rather go to Hell than to take any chance of being in the same place as Pa.

"Well, I don't think you have to worry about that, Martha, because the Old Man is so mean, I don't think he will make it to Heaven," I said. "So you can go ahead and be happy with God in Heaven."

After I went to work in St. Paul, Minnesota, I went back home sometimes on weekends to visit my younger brothers and sisters. On one of my visits, I noticed that Martha had a huge pocket of pus sticking out like a small balloon from the side of her face. I knew right away that it was caused by her mouth full of decayed teeth that were rotting into her gums. She was never taken to a dentist to get them fixed because Pa did not want to spend the money. I couldn't even imagine how much pain Martha suffered from having so many bad teeth. I suggested to Pa that Martha should be taken to a dentist.

"Well, I would take her to a dentist, but she doesn't want to go," Pa said. "Just ask her."

Of course, Martha was told that the dentist had a really long needle, so she was afraid it would hurt more to go to a dentist than it did to endure the pain she had from not going. I wish now that I would have found a way to get Martha to a dentist, even if I had to pay for it out of my own pocket.

The last time I saw Martha alive was during Christmas of 1969. A few months earlier, I had married my U.S. Navy husband, Skip. Fifty sailors were there, but no family members on either side bothered to attend. Therefore, when we were moving from San Diego, California, to Norfolk, Virginia, we decided to stop in Minnesota so I could introduce my husband to my younger siblings. All my brothers were lined up on the sofa, but I noticed that someone was missing.

"Where is Martha?"

I asked the question, but I already knew the answer. Whenever special company came over, Martha was expected to go upstairs and hide. I missed my sister, so I went upstairs and found her. Martha was sitting on the floor sobbing. I gave her a hug and invited her to come downstairs to meet my husband. When I did that, I'll never forget the grateful look on her face just because I treated her like a human being.

It had been two years since I last saw Martha, so I immediately noticed that her complexion looked almost white and I mentioned it to Ma.

"Oh, she always looked like that," Ma said. "You just forgot because you were away so long." With those few comments, the idea that Martha might have needed medical treatment was simply brushed aside.

Before I left, Martha asked me if she could give me a hug goodbye.

"Of course you can," I said. I never realized that I would never be able to hug her again.

About a week before Martha died, I had a strong urge to phone home. We had no cell phones back then, and long-distance phone calls cost a lot of money. It was my policy to call home only for Christmas, Easter, and Mother's Day. Easter had already come and gone because it landed on March 29 in 1970. However, I had a sixth sense that I should call home anyway. Martha answered the phone, and she was very happy I called. She was the only one at home. Everyone else was gone, so I had a long conversation with her. Throughout our conversation, I asked Martha several times if she was feeling okay. She always responded by saying yes. After our conversation ended, Skip asked me why I kept asking Martha if she was feeling well when she kept telling me she was fine.

The next day Skip deployed on a long cruise, so he wasn't there when Pa called a week later.

"I'm calling to tell you Martha died. Her funeral is Saturday. Are you coming?"

I was in shock and could not speak for a few moments. I was trying to comprehend that my nineteen-year-old sister was dead. I did not even know if I had any money in the bank to cover an airline ticket.

"Well, are you coming or not?" Pa asked. "Hurry up and tell me, because this is long distance, and it's costing me money."

I managed to say that I would if I could and that I'd try. When I checked my bank account, I had only $150, which was just enough to buy a round-trip airline ticket. I worried what would happen if my husband came back from his deployment and I was not there when he returned. The Red Cross said they could not give Skip a message because he was only a brother-in-law and not an immediate family member of the deceased, so I decided to just leave a note at the apartment.

Then I realized that maybe nobody notified my brother Mark, who was on his way to Hawaii on a U.S. Navy destroyer. I was the only one who had his latest military address. Because Mark qualified as an immediate family member, I called the Red Cross again to ask them to notify him. I later learned Mark would not have received the news if I had not done that.

A helicopter airlifted Mark from his ship, and he managed to arrive about an hour before Martha's funeral. Thankfully, a friend at my apartment complex gave me a ride to the airport.

Most of the other passengers on the airplane had happy

faces, so I tried to smile, too. The white-haired woman in the pillbox hat was going to her fiftieth high school reunion. The petite blonde-haired girl with the angelic face was going to meet her boyfriend. Even the young man in the starched white shirt collar looked happy.

"I missed my brother's wedding, but at least I'm going to make it in time for the reception, and that's the best part anyway," he said.

The Swedish woman in the aisle seat opened her blouse and openly started to breastfeed her baby. Looking intently over his newspaper, the middle-aged businessman was privately delighted. The righteous-looking woman in the window seat, however, let out a gasp.

"Some women have no modesty," she whispered to me in an indignant voice. But I admired the Swedish woman because she was not like my parents. She was taking care of her child regardless of what other people might think.

When I arrived at the Charles A. Lindbergh Airport in Minneapolis, Minnesota, I could still hear the words Ma often told me, "You must never cry in public, or what will people think?" But it was difficult to keep a happy face, so I felt relieved when the airplane finally landed.

The stewardess smiled and said, "I hope you enjoyed your flight!"

As I walked into the airport terminal, the lady next to me tapped me on the arm and said, "Have a good time now!" I no longer cared what people might think.

"I came to attend my sister's funeral," I said as I looked up at her, and I let a floodgate of tears roll down my cheeks.

After arriving, I met up with my sisters Ann and Pat, and we all took the same Greyhound bus from the Twin Cities to our hometown.

That's when I started hearing some of the awful details of what happened the night Martha died.

Martha was going to clean up the dishes, but she told Ma that she was tired and asked if she could do the dishes in the morning instead. Ma agreed and told Martha she could go to bed early. Normally, the younger boys didn't pay much attention to Martha, but when they went upstairs to go to bed, they heard Martha making strange noises. Matt believes now that the gurgling noises they heard Martha making were probably what are now known as the death rattle. For Matt to be concerned enough to go downstairs to alert my parents said a lot.

When Ma went upstairs to check on Martha, she could not even wake her up by putting cold water on her forehead, but Pa still decided not to take her to the doctor. Nobody could ever go against Pa's decisions without being clobbered, but that night Paul found the courage to do just that, Matt said.

"If you don't take her to the doctor, she will die!" Paul said.

"I was really surprised and proud of Paul for having the courage to stand up to the Old Man," Matt told me. "I thought he would be in serious trouble, but Pa just ignored him and went back to bed."

Matt also heard Pa say, "She would be better off dead."

I later asked Ma about it, and she said that Pa had told her that none of us other children would want to take care of Martha when they were gone, so "she would be better off dead."

I was so angry when I heard that. I would have gladly taken care of Martha, and I know at least four of my other siblings would have done so, too.

Ma told me she wanted to call a doctor, but the phone lines were dead from the heavy snowfall. I asked Missy to send me her recollections of what happened, and this is what she said:

I was only twelve when I found Martha dead. The evening she died, she came in after dumping some scraps to the pigs and said she got a shock from the fence. I remember the Old Man saying that "was a bunch of nonsense." I think those were his last words to her. Martha went to bed early instead of helping with the dishes.

Later on, Matt came downstairs and told Mom that she was making strange noises. (She was.) Mom and I went up and found she hadn't changed into her nightgown, so we helped her change and noticed she was really out of it, not responding to our questions. We moved her from her own bed to mine and went back downstairs.

Mom went in and told the Old Man Martha was sick and needed a doctor. I remember them arguing. He yelled something like, "She'd be better off dead," and he never once checked on her.

Mom came into the kitchen, where all of us kids still at home were gathered, and told us Pa would not let her call Dr. Lee. I remember Matt saying, "She needs a doctor or she'll die." I remember the fear in the room; none of us dared to disobey the tyrant. It was 10 p.m. by then, and we all belonged in bed, but no one wanted to go. I can't speak for anyone else, but I felt so helpless and scared that I stayed on the sofa downstairs in

the living room. I tried to sleep but lay awake all
night worrying and praying for my sick sister and
noticing that neither parent went up during the
night to check on her.

In the morning, the boys went to the barn to
do the chores, and I had to get some things from
my room for school, including an overdue library
book. I knew before I walked in the room that
Martha was dead. She wasn't breathing. Her eyes
were open and glassy, and she had white foam on
her mouth.

I know it sounds weird, but all of my fear left
me the second I saw her. I had this amazing sense
of peace, and I just knew she was in Heaven. I
just stood there for a few seconds in shock, trying
to get my twelve-year-old head around the fact
that my sister was dead at nineteen. I told Ma,
who sent me to the barn to tell the Old Man.
He didn't even stop milking, but told me to have
Ma call Dr. Lee. Of course, by then it was much
too late. Ma, Joey, and I dragged Martha's body
downstairs, still on a mattress.

When Dr. Lee came, he said to call the morgue.
He told us Martha had been dead for hours.

Missy could not remember if Pa made them go to school
that day. What she did not know is that Matt did not go to
the barn to do chores. When he learned that Martha had
died, he said he felt an obligation as the oldest one still living
at home to take care of business and do what had to be done.

Here's the rest of what happened that day, according to
Matt:

I went directly to the garage to get the 22 rifle. I loaded it and started heading toward the barn to kill the Old Man. We didn't need him, because we three boys were already doing most of the work, and we could have run the farm without him, but as I walked toward the barn with the rifle in my hands, I started shaking. I shook so badly that I was afraid I might miss, and then I knew I couldn't do it.

Matt realized that if he killed Pa, he would become part of the very evil that he wanted to get rid of. That's when he decided that he, Buzz, and Paul would have to run away instead. (I wrote about that in the next chapter.)

As for Missy, here's the rest of her story:

I remember feeling numb for weeks after that, probably in shock, going through the motions and asking God why. Why did my father let my sister die? I never got my answer, but I do think God took her up to Heaven so she'd be spared any more pain living under that roof with little hope of leaving, which is the one thing the rest of us had.

I will never be afraid of death again after finding Martha. There was a peaceful presence in that room that I will never forget. I don't know if that experience led me to become a nurse, but I do know it changed me forever. I vowed if I ever had kids, I would never, ever fail in the way the Old Man failed Martha that night.

We all learned something of value during the short time we were blessed to have Martha with us. Pat said it best when she wrote: Martha was a 'choice spirit' whose mission on Earth was to teach the rest of us to be more humble, patient, forgiving, and kind to one another.

I wrote this poem about her.

Martha

Her graduation day
at the young-old age nineteen,
It was Martha's graduation—
not the usual kind you've seen.

I heard her agonizing cry
ring in my ears at night.
A young and frightened child myself,
I could not make it right.

Her teeth decayed into her gums;
her jaw heavy from the pus;
Perhaps the poison numbed her brain,
and she could have been like us.

She was helpful, kind, and cheerful,
but she's retarded they all said;
so ignored and usually hidden,
she died alone in bed.

Her graduation day
in gray coffin and black hearse;
It was Martha's graduation,
and we celebrate the curse.

Matt,
ten years old

Buzz,
nine years old

Paul,
eight years old

RUNAWAY BOYS

By LATE 1970, other than the two youngest, Missy and Joey, Matt, seventeen, Buzz, sixteen, and Paul, fifteen, were the only children left at home to help Pa do the farmwork. Pa could not continue to operate a 400-acre farm without them, but under the circumstances, the three boys decided they could no longer stay until they graduated from high school.

"The drudgery of farmwork was sporadically broken up by the physical and emotional abuse," Buzz said.

Two major family tragedies happened fairly close together that made the situation become even more volatile—the farm fire on September 26, 1967, and the death of Martha on April 23, 1970.

As I discussed in the previous chapter, Pa refused to take Martha to a doctor and just went to bed and let her die. When she was found dead the next morning, something snapped inside Matt. He said he wanted to shoot Pa, but he shook too badly to do it.

"That's when I knew we had only one other option—to run away," Matt said. Matt, Buzz, and Paul put Matt's first plan into action. Here's the story I was told.

By the time school let out for the year, the boys had scraped together three bicycles. After Pa went to bed, about 11 p.m., they climbed out the upstairs window, got onto the garage roof, and jumped to the ground. Then they left on their bikes with a little food, a few clothes, and very little money. Heading toward Minneapolis on Highway 55 East, things were going well for about twenty miles—until the bike tires Buzz was riding started losing air.

"We stopped at a gas station in Brooten to pump up the tire, when a policeman came out," Buzz said.

When the policeman spotted them, he got curious about what three young boys were doing there in the middle of the night, so he started asking questions. The middle one, Buzz, had the most creative gift of gab, so he usually served as the spokesperson for the three boys.

"I told him we were going to visit our cousins in Wayzata, and our father's name was John Smith from Kensington," Buzz said. "He went inside to call our father, and we peddled like hell to the edge of town, where we found cover in an oats field. We dragged our bikes to stay low as search lights went over our heads."

Meanwhile, the three boys had some discussion about their dire situation. It was obvious they could not get very far on their bikes in one night, and they had only a little more than $5. After a half-hour, there was no sign of the policeman, so they made the most logical decision. They would have to go back until they could come up with a better getaway plan.

After peddling their bikes thirty-four miles round-trip to Brooten, the boys made it back to the farm at about 5:30 a.m., collapsing with exhaustion on the living room sofa. A few minutes later, Pa got up to do morning chores and milk the cows.

"Oh, it's nice to see you boys got up early for a change," Pa said. He had no idea they had never gone to bed in the first place. With no sleep at all, Matt, Buzz, and Paul had to find the strength to still do their chores on the farm all day.

"Matt's new plan took a year to materialize," Buzz said. "It took time to get the $75 car, camping gear, and a little money to tide us over between hauling hay jobs we planned to do on the road."

One of the boys worked for another farmer while the other two did the chores for all three of them. As long as the work got done, Pa would not miss them.

"We got paid $1 per hour doing various jobs for another farmer, and then we bought a 1961 Ford Fairlane," Matt said. "We also sold our (Indian) motorcycle."

The boy's second plan to make their great escape in June appeared to be coming along well, but it nearly failed in March.

"After two hours of chores one morning, we were getting ready for the school bus when the Old Man came into the house and told Paul to come downstairs," Buzz said. "He gave Paul a severe beating, saying he didn't do his chores right. Matt and I watched from the top of the stairs. On the bus, Matt and I told Paul we were going to have to kill the Old Man before he killed us."

"No," Paul said. "We only have to make it three more months"—and they did.

They kept their car at a neighbor's house until they were

ready to leave, and this time they were never going back.

I first learned that Matt, Buzz, and Paul had run away when Buzz telephoned me from South Dakota. I was a U.S. Navy spouse living in Norfolk, Virginia. I was so surprised when Buzz told me they even brought their suits in case they decided to attend church on Sunday.

"We went to the Laundromat to wash our clothes, but we forgot to buy detergent," Buzz said. "So we just waited until another lady wasn't looking, and we used some of hers."

"How can you afford to call me long distance?" I asked.

"Because I memorized the Old Man's telephone card number," Buzz said.

"Don't you know he will know where you were when you called me when he gets his bill? You better not use his card anymore, or he might find you."

I learned that Pa put out a national search to find the boys, but they never stayed in one place very long. Whenever they needed more money, they stopped in at various farms to work for a few days. The three of them were such good farmhands that they could easily earn $80 in a single weekend, and then they would move on again. In fact, they traveled to South Dakota, North Dakota, Iowa, Missouri, Kentucky, Tennessee, Indiana, Illinois, Wisconsin, and Minnesota.

"This plan worked well," Buzz said. "We were free and having a 'Huck Finn' type of adventure. I never had to work for the devil again."

During their adventures, the boys stopped in Minneapolis to visit our older sister, Pat, and her late husband Jim, who put them to work laying brick blocks for their new patio deck.

The boys also visited their big brother Bernie in Tennessee.

"I discovered the brakes on their car were in really bad shape," Bernie said. "I did a lot of work on their brakes, so they got a free brake job."

Without help from the three boys, Pa had no choice but to start downsizing the workload he had on the farm. The oldest, Tom, had a farm in Lowry, so he helped Pa out as much as he could. Tom and Joey helped Pa put up more than 6,000 bales of hay from his first crop, and Pa said he "called in" his cows to the National Farmers Organization in St. Cloud, and hauled a load in each evening after milking. It was not a bad time to sell cows. Tom took five of Pa's best cows and sold five of his own cows. Pa wrote in his autobiography that he was through milking in a week, but he said he still had about forty head of the young cattle left.

"Well, we were in a real bind," Pa wrote. "I had lots of cultivating and haying to do and idle tractors sitting around. Two weeks after the boys left, we got a call from a sheriff in Sidney, Iowa. He said the boys had pulled into a park there, and they looked pretty needy to him. I asked him to talk to them and tell them they could come home. He said he would and promised to call back, but he never did."

Pa said he then called that sheriff back again and learned that the boys had told the sheriff some pretty bad "lies" about how they had been treated at home.

"They had high school to finish, but I just didn't bother much more, as it turns you off pretty much to discover your boys have been telling lies about home," Pa said.

At one point the three boys stopped to work for a farmer in South Dakota. I'll call him Duke. After raising their own children, Duke and his wife often cared for foster children, who helped them on their farm. They took an interest in the boys, and when Duke learned they were living in a tent, he offered to let them stay in their guest room.

"You boys look like you could use a hot shower and some

good food in your bellies," Duke said, so he invited them to join them for dinner, too. While they were gathered around the dinner table, Duke pointed to Paul and jokingly said, "I really like this little fellow; I'd like to keep him."

Matt and Buzz immediately put their heads together for a quiet discussion. Then they turned to Duke and said, "Okay, you can have him."

Duke was really surprised when he realized they were actually serious.

The boys told Duke that after they were done with their summer adventure, they would be back to turn over custody of Paul to him because they thought it would be a good idea for Paul to stay there to help him while Paul finished high school. They also told Duke that it would not be safe for Paul to go back home to finish school because Pa abused him too much.

Paul was only fifteen years old, so Duke said, in that case, he would need to get legal guardianship over Paul as his foster child, and that's what Duke and his wife did, with the help of Social Services and our sister Pat. After Pat verified Paul's abusive situation, he got a brand-new, safe place to live.

In spite of the fact that Duke and his wife were, more or less, pulled out of a grab bag, they turned out to be very good foster parents and really helped Paul a lot with his schoolwork.

"I started trying to locate Paul and found out where he was," Pa said. "But I just dropped the idea of getting him back when I discovered how much he wanted to be away from home."

When my husband, infant son, and I went to Minnesota to visit Ma and my youngest siblings in 1971, we decided to go a little farther and visit Paul in South Dakota. I found Duke and his wife to be very nice people, and Paul was glad that we visited when we did. At that time, his foster parents were thinking of sending Paul back home; however, they changed their minds when I confirmed the horrible abuse that Paul would most likely have to face.

As for Matt and Buzz, they went to live on our big brother Tom's farm in Lowry. Because Lowry did not have a high school, they were able to return to the same high school in Glenwood until they graduated, too.

"When we ran away, we were very successful," Matt said. "Remember to put that in your book. We were successful runaways because none of us three boys ever had to go back and work for Pa again."

At first I wondered why that part of this story was so important to Matt, but now I think I figured it out: Matt, Buzz, and Paul were the first and only siblings who were able to come up with a plan and stand up to the Old Man, saying, "Enough, already; we refuse to be victims of your abuse anymore. No more beatings and no more child abuse."

That is indeed an important message for all victims. Somebody has to find the courage to stand up and put a stop to all forms of abuse and bullying, one way or another.

Was it difficult for Ma when three of her sons ran away? Yes, because she worried a lot about them. I telephoned her to tell her they were fine, but none of us older siblings would tell either one of our parents where they were.

Was it difficult for Pa? Yes, definitely, because he could not do all of the farmwork without those three boys. Pa even had to hire help for the first time to harvest the oats. Here's what Pa had to say about it:

I put the farm up for sale at a low, low price.
The agent's brother, another agent, bought it in
September. Then I got busy looking for another,
smaller farm. October 10, after an early snow-
storm on very dry ground, I found the place
at Dalton. I took Ma (Missy, Joey, and two of
Tom's children) to see it. They all liked it a lot.
Then we closed the deal, and I started plowing
it. The weather got wetter and wetter, and I did
not quite finish the plowing. I moved grain and
machinery through the winter, and just before
April 1971, we moved furniture and hogs and
three big loads, forty-seven head, of young cattle.
Then a couple loads of ear corn, and that was
done. Then I went to buy smaller machinery, and
(Tom) kept stuff like the four-row corn planter
and twelve-foot drill.

Some of us older children often thought about running away, too, but we were too concerned about how badly it might impact our younger siblings. Therefore, we could not bring ourselves to do it. After the boys ran away, Missy said Pa hired some help, and our oldest brother, Tom, who had another farm in Lowry, helped a lot, too. However, the two youngest, who were twelve and eleven at the time, were made to do much more than was appropriate for their ages and skill sets to harvest crops that year.

In fact, that is the saddest part of this story, as told by Missy, who was left behind:

Pa put me on the tractor a lot to steer when they
baled hay and whatnot. He never explained

anything, even where the brakes were, and I was
scared to death every time I had to do it. If I
screwed up, he would pull me off the tractor and
spank me and yell and scream, which made me so
upset I usually did worse after that. To this very
day, I will not drive a tractor or anything resem-
bling one because that fear comes right back and
grabs me in the chest.

I also remember trying to get hogs and cattle
in the truck to be sold. I was supposed to herd
them in place, but I was a scrawny twelve-year-
old afraid of the large animals. I thought I would
be trampled every time.

I can relate to what Missy is saying here because oftentimes I also had to help load hogs and cattle in the truck to
be hauled and sold at the South St. Paul stockyards. Sometimes as a small ten- to sixteen-year-old girl, I had to hold a
gate near the back of the truck. Pa would chase the animals
toward me and then yell for me to let an animal in or keep an
animal out, and I was so afraid of falling down and getting
trampled. That was really a more appropriate job for somebody like Rambo or the Incredible Hulk, not a young girl,
but this part is Missy's story, and she continued ...

Another memory is being placed in the back of
the big truck when the threshing of oats began. I
was given a big shovel and told to push the grain
around to even it out. But the grain was being
dumped in so fast, I couldn't keep up. Then the
dust from the grain got so bad, I couldn't breathe.
I thought I would suffocate, so I dropped the

shovel and crawled to the top of the truck, coughed, and took a deep breath of air. Pa saw me and stopped the threshing machine and came over and pushed me back in the truck and said I had to keep shoveling or get buried by the oats. I believed that may just happen, and I still don't know how I survived that day. I know Joey was put in similar situations that summer.

I remember lifting big bales and working so hard physically that I slept long hours and woke up not knowing what time it was or where I was. I think I blocked out a lot about that summer because it was the scariest time of my life.

I wished the older boys had taken me with them when they ran away, but I understood why they couldn't do it, and I was happy that they escaped. I was so relieved when I learned that we were moving to a smaller farm because the workload wasn't as bad there. Pa still made us work a lot, and he was still abusive, mostly verbally abusive, but I stayed after school and got involved in sports and anything to stay away from him. The elementary school principal hired me (through a government-sponsored CETA program) to help him with typing and filing for an hour or two after school most days of the week. This gave me money to buy things like basketball shoes and my majorette boots for marching band.

Looking back now, as an adult, I wonder why Social Services didn't come out and assess the safety of Joey and me and put us in foster care,

too. But maybe back then the programs weren't
as developed as they are today.

It breaks my heart to learn what my youngest sister, Missy, and brother, Joey, had to go through after Matt, Buzz, and Paul left. But did I blame them for leaving? No, because they did what they felt they had to do, and Missy did not blame them either.

"I don't hold any hostility toward those older boys for leaving because their lives were even more of a hell than mine," Missy said. "I was happy for them that they got away. We all just wanted to get out alive."

By the time Pa found out where the boys were located, he had already downsized, so he just gave up on getting them back home.

Sometimes we children learned we just had to stick together. We did that a lot. Having the support of each other probably was our saving grace that helped us survive.

"The emotional scars took a lot of time to heal," Buzz said. "I am very healthy and happy now."

All three runaway boys changed their names.

Joey, age three, and Missy, age four, by a shrine Pa built in our yard at the farm in Glenwood. Pa bought the statue of the holy family in St. Cloud, Minnesota.

THE POWER
OF
FORGIVENESS

MANY OF US FIND it extremely difficult to forgive people who have abused or wronged us in any way, shape, or form. But for our own good, it's so much better if we do.

Ma often said, "Before you judge others, walk a mile in their shoes."

My son Shawn said, "I can tell you two good reasons why we should walk a mile in someone else's shoes. First, you will then be a mile away from that other person. Second, that other person will no longer have shoes." Of course, that's not what Ma meant, so I took her advice by trying to put myself in my parents' shoes.

Two days after graduating from high school, I left on a train from the nearest train station from my hometown of 3,000 and headed to the big city of St. Paul, Minnesota. I felt confident that where I was going had to be better than what I was leaving, but all I had was $6, the "Best Typist of the Year" award in my pocket, a pair of ice skates around my neck, and one small weekend suitcase that was half full of clothes and half full of books. Unfortunately, I also took some extra baggage with me that I didn't know I had—memories of abuse, feelings of hatred, and other unresolved issues.

In fact, I felt very much like Humpty Dumpty, who *"sat on a wall because just like Humpty Dumpty I felt like I had a great fall, and all the king's horses and all the king's men couldn't put (me) back together again."* I spent the next several years trying to put my own broken self together again. My new mission was to heal my inner wounds and create a happier me, but that didn't happen (and probably couldn't happen) until I learned how to forgive.

I first started working on the issue of forgiveness when I was in my midtwenties. I read a little piece of wisdom I found in a tabloid magazine (of all places). In a nutshell, the article said that the greatest gift we have to give to another person is the gift of our time—and it takes a lot of time to do an effective job of hating someone. Therefore, "Why would we give the gift of our time to someone we hate?" That question really resonated with me. I thought about it long and hard.

The article emphasized how holding hatred and grudges toward another person does more harm to the beholder of such ill feelings than to anyone else. It compared holding on to grudges and hatred to having cancer—a cancer that grows and grows on the inside until it completely destroys the grudge-holder's health.

That's when I started reading what the Bible says about forgiveness. The first verse that came to mind was Matthew 6:14-15—*"For if you forgive others their trespasses, your heavenly Father will also forgive you; but if you do not forgive others, neither will your Father forgive your trespasses.*" When I read that, I said to my Bible study companion, "Holy cow! That does not give us any other options. We have no choice but to forgive our enemies. That means I even have to forgive my father."

I had already forgiven Ma. After walking a mile in her shoes, I saw how she was also a victim. Ma grew up pampered and spoiled. Grandma said whenever Ma threw a temper tantrum as a child, her dad always gave in, and she got her own way. When she married Pa, however, throwing temper tantrums no longer worked. Whenever she threw temper tantrums, Pa slapped her down and beat her up. I think that after enduring many years of that kind of abuse, Ma just gave up and stopped trying to stand up to him.

Ma was a hard worker, and she was strong in some ways, but emotionally Ma was very weak. Having so many children would be extremely difficult for any woman, especially a victim of spousal abuse. I know Ma was under a tremendous amount of stress, so it's not surprising that she had some temporary emotional breakdowns.

In those days, I had never heard of people being treated for bipolar conditions or people taking medicine to control or prevent depression. Mental health issues and services were never talked about, at least not in our small town, but that doesn't mean nobody suffered from those conditions.

Ma often told me in later conversations that she wished she would have done things differently. I believe Ma loved all of us children and did the best she could at the time.

During her last few years of life, when Ma was in her nineties, she was tormented by her memories of Katherine's untimely death as a three-month-old baby, and she also regretted that she did not find a way to get Martha to a doctor.

That might have been impossible without Pa's help because there was a lot of snow on the ground and Ma could not drive, but she still blamed herself.

My sister Ann told me that she could never forgive Ma because if she were in her shoes, she would have done so much better. As I think about that now, I wonder how she could possibly know. Ann was never pregnant, but Ma was pregnant seventeen times; Ann earned a doctorate's degree, but Ma only went to school through eighth grade; Ann had a driver's license, but Ma never learned to drive; Ann had access to books and the information superhighway, but Ma never did. Therefore, under exactly the same circumstances, how could Ann possibly know for sure she would have done any better than Ma? In fact, I do not think it would be fair for any of us girls to say that. We might all *think* we could have, and would have, done better than our mother did, but we can never really know for sure. That would be like comparing a basset hound with a German shepherd and expecting both dogs to leap the same six-foot fence.

Did Ma make mistakes? Yes. Did Ma often fail to protect us? Yes. But did Ma do the best she could under the circumstances, despite her inability to cope and lack of skills? Yes, I think she did most of the time, and none of us can ever do better than our best.

Forgiving my father took longer because trying to walk a mile in Pa's shoes was a lot more difficult. I know Pa worried a lot about money. Going through the Great Depression definitely had an impact on him. Why else would he put money in five different banks, hide money in tin cans and jars all over the farm, and complain about every dime he had to spend?

I also know that when people feel guilty, they often strike out at those closest to them. In reality, they are angry with themselves, and I'm sure some of Pa's anger came from his feelings of guilt over his mother's death. He knew the motorcycle accident that killed his mother was really his fault. It must have been difficult for him to live with that guilt every day of his life. Whenever Pa was beating us, I wondered if he felt like he was really beating himself for all the wrongs he had done.

I don't think things like anger-control classes were available back then, but I doubt Pa would have accepted that kind of help anyway.

Farmers cannot afford to get sick or take time off because they have to milk cows and feed livestock every day. To me and most of my brothers and sisters, Pa appeared to be as strong as Paul Bunyan's blue ox. I never thought Ma would outlive Pa by nearly twenty-nine years, because it was Ma who was frequently on the verge of death, not Pa. I don't remember Pa ever going to the hospital or seeing a doctor, except to get a huge splinter taken out of his forehead once. I believe he also went to a doctor when he got attacked and badly mauled by a bull. That was the result of his foolishness.

Pa frequently bragged about how friendly and harmless Orgie the bull was, saying he was as tame as a big kitten. Pa was in the pen one night with Orgie, the friendly bull. As Pa was feeding him some hay, he used his pitchfork to lightly scratch Orgie on the back. That was Pa's way of petting the bull. However, Orgie did not like being scratched on the back with a pitchfork. Suddenly, the bull charged at Pa and pinned him against the barn wall. Pa yelled for help, but my brothers had already finished their chores and left. In Pa's struggle to get free from the bull's hold, he pulled on the ring in Orgie's nose, which caused the bull to back off. Then Pa managed to get out of the pen. When Pa reached the house, he collapsed on the kitchen floor. That's all I remember about it.

Pa never bragged about Orgie the friendly bull again. He still led Orgie out into the yard to eat grass, but he used a much longer rope and a much bigger and stronger stake to anchor him to the ground. Pa also never walked with the bull to his back again, either. After Orgie attacked him, he walked far to one side and never took his eyes off the bull, so I know Pa no longer trusted Orgie the friendly bull like he once did.

Even when Pa was attacked by the bull, however, I never remember Pa being sick in bed. I knew he had a hernia and wore a truss to hold his bulging hernia in place. I knew he suffered some pain after doing a lot of heavy lifting, which all farmers had to do on a daily basis in those days. I did not know Pa had two hernias until I read his autobiography, which I still have in his own handwriting. This is what he wrote:

> From age thirty on to about sixty-four, all but
> one-and-one-half years, I had one hernia, and for
> about ten years I had two, and never had time
> to get them fixed. So I had to use and wear out
> several trusses. When the workload lightened, the
> last one healed shut, a wonderful relief.

I also was aware that sometimes Pa had backaches, but I never knew how much he suffered from them. Here's what Pa wrote about it:

> For over thirty years while farming, I had lots of
> backaches. Sometimes for over a year in a spell,
> not a pain-free minute. I ate many meals (from a

*plate) off the floor while I lay on the sofa because
I couldn't stand to sit at the table. Sometimes I
couldn't sleep for several weeks from pain. Doctors never helped, but dentists did several times.
No doubt, this made my disposition sour, and the
family did not know why I was crabby.*

Admitting that he had a "sour" disposition with a "crabby" personality was putting it lightly. Pa's explosive temper
and physical abuse were terrifying. For a man who suffered
from so much pain, where did he get the physical strength
and energy to beat the hell out of us kids so often? If I were in
severe physical pain, that's the last thing I'd be doing.

While Pa's worries about money, feelings of guilt, and pain
might very well have had a lot to do with his uncontrollable
outbursts of anger, they're a poor excuse for abusing one's
own wife and children to the extent that he did. That's why I
highly suspect his problems ran much deeper than the physical pain he endured. No doubt, Pa had some serious mental
health issues, too.

Some of my siblings spent thousands of dollars on coun-
seling sessions in an effort to come to terms with all of the
abuse they suffered. My brother Paul telephoned me one day
and asked me a strange question. He said his therapist asked
him, "If you could do anything you wanted to do to your dad
to punish him for what he did to you, what would you like
to do? What could you do to him that would make you feel
good?

"I would like to throw a fresh cowpie in the Old Man's
face," Paul said. His therapist then told him to call all of his
siblings and ask each of us if we would like to do the same.
By that time, I had already dealt with most of my feelings

of hatred. I don't know how my other siblings responded, but I said, "No, because I wouldn't want to waste the time or energy." If I were asked that same question later, I might have said, "I would just like to hear him say how wrong he was, how deeply sorry he was, and beg for my forgiveness." Unfortunately, Pa passed away without ever giving any of us that kind of satisfaction. He never admitted that he abused us, but in his autobiography, he did admit he was "very hard on" us kids. Pa wrote:

> *The reason I was so hard on the kids is because this world is tough, and I wanted them to be tough enough to take whatever life threw their way without leaning on drugs or alcohol for a crutch.*

If that's what he intended to do, I guess he succeeded, because most of us are tough enough to deal with some very difficult life situations. However, Pa crossed the line from discipline to abuse in the first degree far too often, and there is a huge difference between being "very hard on" children and abusing them. Perhaps Pa did have some regrets near the end of his life, when he wrote:

> *As I look back, I often wish I could have taken a different road in life and maybe do better ... As long as we are human, we will make mistakes, and we can't go back and right the wrongs. We can only go ahead and continue to try to do better. At present time I am 68½ years old and probably won't add more to my life story.*

Two weeks later, Pa passed away from a massive bee-sting-related heart attack, but before he did, he gave Ma his autobiography and told her to give it to me when she came out west with Mark and his family because "Barbara is the writer in the family."

After I became an adult, I never blamed my parents for anything. Once I was free from their control, I had the power to change whatever I didn't like to make a better and happier life for myself. If I failed to do so, it was my fault, not theirs. If I could not do any better or make better choices than my parents did, then I could not blame them for not doing better either.

I always felt it was a sorry excuse when forty-year-olds still blame their parents for their own mistakes and failures. I would say to those people, "Take a good look in the mirror and grow up. Plenty of people who have been abused and had terrible parents still managed to get a good education, build highly successful careers, and become contributing members of society."

I read that one in every four Americans has been a victim of child abuse. Thank God, my siblings and I, as well as many other victims of child abuse, found enough strength of character to take charge of our lives and rose above it.

One thing I had in my favor is that I've always been an avid reader and writer. I love reading books, magazines, and newspapers. The more I read, the more I learned, and that played a huge part in my ability to overcome my abusive childhood. In fact, I believe my journal writing was my greatest therapy. It took a long time before I felt like a whole person again, but whenever I compared my adult life with my childhood, everything always seemed so much easier.

When I got my first full-time job as a secretary for

Minnesota State Parks, for instance, I felt more like I was on vacation. I couldn't believe I was actually getting paid to have such an easy life—just sitting in a fancy chair inside an air-conditioned office, answering the phone, taking Gregg stenography dictation, and doing some simple typing. That was far better than doing slave labor in the hot sun on the farm for no money at all.

I read that it is easier to forgive someone for abuse if we can feel grateful for the lessons we learned from it and focus on that. I am grateful that my difficult childhood helped me to develop strong survival instincts and sharp creative skills that I might not have had otherwise. Nothing was handed to me. I had to work for everything I got, so that no doubt made it easier for me to go out and get a job to support myself. No matter how tight the job market was, I always found a way.

For example, when I applied for a position at a high-risk car insurance company, the competition was tough, with several applicants for one job opening. Someone told me that to get a job interview, it's a good idea to put something on the application to make it stand out from all the others. While filling out the application, I kept that in mind and looked for a way I could make some of my answers differ-ent. When it came to "father's occupation," I wrote down "Big Deal Farmer." The next day, I got a call to come in for an interview with Ernie Crust, office manager at Northland Insurance Company in St. Paul, Minnesota. While looking at my application, he said, "I'll be honest with you. The main reason I called you in for this interview is because you wrote down here that your father is a 'Big Deal Farmer,' and I never heard of that. Could you explain it to me?" I smiled and said, "Sure, my father is a farmer, and he thinks it's a big deal, so that makes him a 'Big Deal Farmer.'"

Crust broke out laughing so hard I thought he would fall out of his chair, and he hired me on the spot.

Perhaps the most important thing I learned about forgiveness is that when we forgive others, we are really giving ourselves a gift. Forgiveness is a choice all victims have, regardless of how severe the abuse was.

Below are examples of three victims of extreme abuse who tell their stories about how they forgave their abusers and why:

- Eva Mozes Kor, a Holocaust survivor, forgave Dr. Josef Mengele, who used her and her twin sister for human experiments in Auschwitz. It took fifty years for her to realize that as a victim of the Holocaust, she had the power to forgive.

  "No one could give me that power," she said. "No one could take it away. It was mine to use in any way I wished ... We cannot change what happened, but we can change how we relate to it."

- Dean Eric Smith forgave his stepfather Bob, who beat his mother to death with a baseball bat. Dean was just a boy in fourth grade when he lost both of his parents—his mother was murdered, and his stepdad went to prison. I remember seeing the news on TV when it happened, not far from where I live. Luckily, Dean was adopted by a pastor and his wife. Eventually, Dean became a pastor, too, but he struggled for many years with feelings of hatred when all he wanted to do was kill Bob for killing his mother. While telling his story to a singles' group I attended, Dean carried another man around on his back to demonstrate what a heavy load he carried until he finally summoned enough courage to forgive Bob in person. When he forgave Bob, he got rid of that extra load on his back, but it took him twenty-two years to do it. Dean's powerful and inspirational story is now on a DVD called *Live to Forgive*.

- Elizabeth Smart forgave her abuser, Brian David Mitchell, who kidnapped her at knifepoint in Salt Lake City, Utah, and raped her at the young age of fourteen. After holding Elizabeth in captivity for nine months, Mitchell and his accomplice, Wanda Barzee, were caught and sent to prison. When Elizabeth was reunited with her family, her mother told her that she could never get back those nine months that were stolen from her, but she should not allow her abuser to steal any more. Therefore, the best thing she could do would be to move on and give herself permission to enjoy a full and happy life, so that's what Smart did. She is now married and the mother of three beautiful children—Cloe, James, and Olivia.

All of these victims of severe abuse forgave their abusers. It took Eva fifty years, Dean twenty-two years, and Elizabeth a much shorter time, but they all reported feeling so much better after forgiving them. If they could forgive their abusers, I believe the rest of us should be able to do the same.

Once I grasped the concept of forgiving others as a gift to myself—as something I needed to do for my own good mental health—my healing process began. Forgiveness seldom happens overnight, as seen in these three examples. Sometimes it takes a long time and requires a lot of hard work, but the sooner we can forgive others, the better we will feel.

It's important to know that forgiving others does not mean that we ever have to put up with any more abuse, nor does it mean we will forget what our abusers did. For instance, I cannot get through a single day of my life without remembering what my father did with a table knife. Every time I have a meal and see a table knife, I remember Pa holding my little toddler hands down on the high chair tray and pounding my knuckles with the heavy end of the knife because I could not swallow my lumpy oatmeal fast enough to please him.

Some memories will always be there. Forgiving our abusers also does not mean we will ever allow them to hurt us again. We can, and always should, stay away from toxic and abusive people.

The bottom line is that we are who we are for a reason. Many times parents who abuse their children were also abused by their own parents. That does not excuse this kind of behavior, but it does help explain why it happened, and why it continues to happen. To put an end to this vicious cycle of dysfunctional families, where the abused often become the abusers, we must first fix ourselves so we can purposely do what we need to do to stop it. We cannot change our beginnings, but we can change our endings. Thank God for that.

Perhaps the most important thing to remember is that each and every one of us can make a positive difference in the lives of others—in particular, in the lives of those who might be in abusive relationships right now. We never know when a simple act of kindness, a few positive words of encouragement, a smile, or a loving hug could make a difference—one person at a time. What could be better than that?

I wrote a poem titled *Writing with Passion* that partly explains how I was able to turn my abusive childhood into a positive experience and become a better person.

WRITING WITH PASSION

I write with passion about child abuse prevention because a man grabbed me and held a gun to my head when I was five years old.

I write with passion about spouse abuse prevention because I saw my father beat my mother, and I heard her screams for help.

I write with passion about suicide prevention because I could not save my good friend and neighbor who took her own life.

I write with passion about the struggles of single parents because I felt the agony of divorce and raised my sons alone.

I write with passion about substance abuse prevention because a family member is a recovering addict who nearly lost his life.

I write with passion about the value of education because I earned my bachelor's degree as a single parent with three part-time jobs.

I write with passion about the importance of a work ethic because that made it possible for me to reach my goals for a better life.

I write with passion about making a difference and helping others because my friends were always there when I needed them most.

I write with passion about setting goals and daring to dream because sometimes goals and dreams might be all we have left.

I write with passion about believing in ourselves, God, and Country because I value my freedom and I have seen miracles.

I write with passion because I have seen that, been there, heard that, felt that—and all of those moments left a mark in the center of my heart.

I live with passion, and I will not allow anyone to put me down because I'm mighty proud of the person I am in spite of where I have been.

I have been to hell and back ... but I thank God for my struggles because they have given me more strength and empathy than most people will ever know.

Mark distinguished himself with a very impressive military career as a Blackhawk pilot in command, with 5,000 hours of accident-free flying. This did not surprise me because Mark was always mechanically gifted and could already drive Pa's big truck on dirt farm roads at age 8.

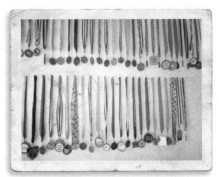

Since Age 55, Mark won more than 80 medals and trophies for gold, silver, and bronze place finishes in 5K running competitions.

I received the Superior Award for Civilian Service medals once and the U.S. Army's Commander's Award for Superior Service medals three times

My sister Pat when she was a finalist in the Miss Minneapolis pageant

I received the Thomas Jefferson Award twice for best newspaper in all four branches of the military, beating out more than 6,000 other military newspapers competing in the same category.

WHERE THEY ARE NOW

CONSIDERING WHAT ALL TWELVE of us surviving children have been through, we have all done well as adults. All twelve of us are well educated, and eight of the twelve earned a four-year college degree or higher. Six of my seven brothers served in the military. Eight of us are officially retired, but most of us still have part-time jobs. All of us had, or still have, successful careers. In fact, most of us have won top awards in our career fields. Perhaps we were all trying to prove to our parents and ourselves that we are better and have more worth than the earthworms we dug. Ten of us twelve are now grandparents.

1. **Tom** graduated from high school, joined the U.S. Air Force, and graduated from a 44-week course and became a munitions expert. He spent four years in the air force loading every type of munitions on board all sorts of aircraft, including bombs on B-52s. He also worked as a farmer and held multiple management positions in the National Farmers Organization, including serving as the national director. He has four children and one stepdaughter. He is married and lives in Minnesota.

2. **Bernie** earned his GED and went to vocational-technical school for welding and brick masonry. He attended North Dakota State College of Science in Wahpeton, North Dakota, and St. Louis Community College, where he studied law enforcement procedures. He worked as a welder, a farmer, and a security guard at the St. Louis Arch in Missouri. He also served in the U.S. Army as a paratrooper. He has three children. He has been married for fifty-three years and lives in Illinois.

3. **Pat** graduated from high school and then attended the MacPhail School of Music for two years. Because of her singing talent, she was a finalist in the Miss Minneapolis Pageant. She studied at Anne Arundel Community College in Maryland. She worked as an insurance claims representative for Marquette National Bank. Pat has one son and one stepdaughter. She is a widow and resides in Maryland.

4. **Rose** graduated from high school and earned her BA in education from the College of St. Benedict in St. Joseph, Minnesota. She became a nun and lived in a convent for seven years. She also worked as a teacher, bank loan processor, day care teacher, and nanny. She has two children. She has been married for forty-six years and lives in Minnesota.

5. **I** graduated from high school and earned my BA in English-writing (journalism) from the University of Puget Sound in Tacoma, Washington. I also completed the Public Affairs Officer course at Fort Benjamin Harrison in Indiana. I have worked as a secretary,

the owner of a licensed child care business, a newspaper reporter, editor, photojournalist, public affairs officer, comedian, blog writer, and author. I have two sons and three stepdaughters. I am single and reside in Washington state.

6. **Ann** graduated from high school and St. Catherine University (St. Kate's) in St. Paul, Minnesota, with a BA in education. She then earned her MA and PhD at the University of Minnesota. She worked as a teacher and a principal, and is now a world traveler. She has two stepchildren. She is single, but is engaged and lives in Florida.

7. **Mark** graduated from high school and the University of Minnesota-Morris, where he received a BA in sociology, with a minor in economics. He is also a graduate of the thirteen-month Rotary Wing Helicopter School. He worked as a Blackhawk Pilot in Command, with 5,000 hours of accident-free flying. He is also a Commissioned Chief Warrant Officer. He has completed extensive military service, including thirteen years in the U.S. Navy, where he worked on a light cruiser and destroyer and completed three West-Pac cruises to Vietnam. He also served for thirteen years in the U.S. Army, including thirteen months in the Persian Gulf War. He has one daughter. He has been married for forty-five years and resides in Minnesota.

8. **Matt** is a high school graduate and a graduate of Minnesota State University Moorhead, with a bachelor's of science degree in accounting. He worked as an

accountant for eighteen years and as a truck driver. He also served in the U.S. Navy, working as a Nuclear Missile Launch Technician for four years aboard the navy's submarines. He has two children and three stepchildren. He is married and lives in Minnesota.

9. **Buzz** graduated from high school and earned a BA in education from the University of St. Thomas in St. Paul, Minnesota. He attended eight colleges and universities and earned an MA in business education. He has had an extensive career that included working for ten years as a restaurant manager at Perkins (where he earned the Best Manager of the Year in the United States award), teaching (in two colleges, twenty-two high schools, thirty-four middle schools, two elementary schools, and the Sylvan Learning Center), and owning and operating a house painting business. He has two children. He is single but has a significant other and resides in Minnesota.

10. **Paul** graduated from high school in South Dakota. He is also a graduate of Alexandria Technical and Community College in Minnesota (AA in hydraulics) and Dunwoody College of Technology in Minneapolis (electrical). In addition to working as a security guard, he worked as an electrician for thirty years. He served in the U.S. Navy for four years aboard submarines as a machinist mate. He has one daughter. He has been married for thirty-nine years and lives in Minnesota.

11. **Missy** graduated from high school and then went on to earn her BA in nursing from St. Catherine University (St. Kate's) in St. Paul, Minnesota. She also earned

a master's degree in public health from the University of Minnesota. She is an RN and an occupational health specialist. She has two children and two step-children. She is married and resides in New York.

12. **Joey** is a high school graduate and a graduate of Alexandria Technical and Community College in Minnesota (accounting and business management). He works as an electrician and a supervisor at 3M. He also served in the U.S. Navy for twelve years on submarines. He has two children and one stepchild. He is married and lives in Minnesota.

ABOUT THE AUTHOR

BARBARA SELLERS was the sixth born in a family of fourteen children. She grew up on a large farm in Minnesota.

Barbara decided to become a writer when she was nine years old. At large family gatherings, her grandmother got everyone's attention and read humorous parts of Barbara's letters aloud. Everyone laughed and applauded, so she continued writing. When she wrote to a Japanese pen pal, Barbara unwittingly developed stronger writing skills. Knowing her pen pal had to interpret her letters into a foreign language forced her to pay attention to correct spelling and better sentence structure.

After graduating from high school, Barbara worked as a secretary in St. Paul, Minnesota, for a few years before moving to Tacoma, Washington, to escape the cold weather. There she met her first husband, the late Franklin Harvey, who was a sonar technician in the U.S. Navy. After living in several naval ports throughout the United States, Barbara earned a bachelor's degree in English-writing (journalism) in May 1982 from the University of Puget Sound in Tacoma, Washington, where she now resides.

Barbara retired in May 2009 from the Department of Defense, where she worked for an Army newspaper, the *Northwest Guardian,* as a reporter, editor, and photojournalist in the public affairs office. While there, she wrote more than 4,000 stories and won thirty-two Keith L. Ware individual and staff journalism awards, including the coveted Thomas Jefferson Award twice, for best newspaper out of more than 6,000 in all four branches of the military.

Barbara is a thirty-year member of Toastmasters International and has won many humorous speech contests. After retirement, she did some stand-up comedy at open mikes and has two humorous CDs of original true stories, *True Confessions* and *Back on the Farm.* Barbara is also a special guest on the CD *Panic to Power,* with three world champion speakers from Toastmasters. *Get Tough or Die* is Barbara's first novel.

She has two adult sons, Shawn and Ryan, and one granddaughter, Crystal.

ACKNOWLEDGMENTS

SPECIAL THANKS to everyone who generously gave of their time to provide firsthand information, suggestions, and/ or editorial corrections or helped verify facts with research: Crystal N. Harvey, Donald R. Sellers, Billie Stewart, Patricia Seger, William Wolfram, Jennifer Pittz, Steve Pawlitschek, Peter Blumer, James Love, Rev. Dr. Robert Sullivan, Tobin Stewart, James Rogers, Fredrick Zwiefel, Jennifer Bright Reich, Christina Gaugler, Amy Kovalski, and Attorney Ross Brandborg.

I am also grateful to reletives, neighbors, teachers, and friends who made a positive difference in my early life: Marian Brewster, Virginia Scott, Florence Andert, Mary Irgens, Betty Bradfield, Mel Halverson, Lee Paulson, Ron and Ethel Skoog, Marsha Rust Kuschel, Rose Fiala Searcy, Judy Douvier Ziemer, Joyce Hoplin Shea, Lyndah Wallin, Bonnie Halverson, Marjorie Christenson, Barbara Gandrud Ask, Rose Mrnak Danielson, Tommy Riesselman, and Genevieve Murtaugh.

A NOTE FROM THE AUTHOR

BY TELLING MY STORY, I hope readers will be inspired to do whatever they can to help prevent spouse and child abuse. If you know a child is being abused, call the National Child Abuse Hotline at 1-800-4-A-Child (1-800-422-4453). To report domestic violence, call the National Domestic Violence Hotline at 1-800-799-7233 or TTY 1-800-787-3224.

To contact the author, e-mail
GetToughorDieBook@gmail.com
or jenniferreich@momosapublishing.com.

OUTSTANDING BOOK REVIEWS

I really think this book is going to help people with their journey in life. This story is a captivating and very real look into the trauma's surrounding domestic violence.

—James R.

In her riveting book, Barbara clearly does not put her focus on her often, life-threatening plight as much as her unyielding determination, which inspires us all. Barbara is an amazing example that all of us have the resilience of spirit and capability to better ourselves no matter what the odds. One's life can be forever changed for the better after valiantly living through the eyes of Barbara in *Get Tough or Die*.

—Patricia S.

Barbara grew up in the era that "a man's home is his castle." No one questioned the king's rules, as he controlled everything. Barbara captures how creative a sadistic person with a large family can be. This was her father. Her book tells of dangerous situations he put children in when they were way too young, with never a concern for their safety. The book challenges our senses of right and wrong and causes us to weep at the injustices they all went through.

—Billie S.

Barbara was a classmate, and I had met her father once as a child when he delivered hay to our farm. I am aghast upon reading of her and her sibling's emotional and physical abuse. I am extremely proud of Barbara for sharing their story and for learning and showing forgiveness! I couldn't put the book down! I ordered a copy each for my six children to share our local history. Thanks, Barbara for sharing!

—Fred Z.

I loved this book. It was so true and well written. All characters in the book went on to do great things in their lives, even with their upbringing. I married Mark, and he is the best husband, father, and grandpa.

—Pennie P.

I found this book very captivating and could not put it down once I started reading. It was brutally sad but also taught me some lessons to carry forward in my life. First always treat all people with respect and kindness because we don't know what they have going on in their lives. You may be the only nice person in their life that day. Secondly have a forgiving spirit because forgiveness is a not only a command from God but also a gift to yourself. I enjoyed the book very much.

—Dawn P.

Barbara was a classmate of mine. It's so hard to believe the physical and emotional abuse that Barbara and her siblings suffered. You never know what goes on in someone else's life. The forgiveness that Barbara has displayed has made her the strong and kind person she is today. It's a very emotional and captivating story, and it's hard to put down.

—Judy Z

You are a fighter. I can't believe you went through all that and came out such a positive person. I couldn't stop reading your book once I had gotten started. I just finished it, and I'm still in mild shock. I feel two things: I have so much admiration for you for going through these experiences and coming out positive, strong, and independent. Just wow. I don't think I could have done it like that. Secondly, I feel so much gratitude that I have had such an incredibly easy and loving upbringing, none of which is of my own doing. Thank you for writing this book.

—William W.

This book was so riveting; I did not want to put it down. Barb and her family members experienced continuous abuse while growing up. I can't even imagine being treated as such and coming out a successful, award winning person, who forgave her parents for the abuse. Kudos to Barb for being brave and strong enough to share her story, paying tribute to her deceased sisters, being a forgiving person, and for inspiring others to end abuse. Her poem at the end of the book is so inspiring. Thank you, Barb, for being open, caring, and positive, and for encouraging everyone to show simple acts of kindness to others.

—Sue A.